Shih Tzu

about pets

A guide to selection, care, nutrition, rearing, training, health, breeding, sports and play. A must for both owners and people who are interested in finding a suitable dog breed.

P.O. Box 26, 9989 ZG Warffum, the Netherlands
www.aboutpets.info
E-mail: management@aboutpets.info

ISBN: 9789058218162

First edition 2009
Second edition 2010
Third edition 2011

Photos: About Pets photography team

Acknowledgements:
Photos: Brigitta Binnendijk, Silvia van de Meer, Aukie Denie, Melanie vd Berg, Joyce van Dijk, Riet van der Steen and Chantal Roll-Bekkers
Anatomic illustrations: Hill's
Graphs: Courtesy of Royal Canin

Contents

Foreword

The book you are holding is a basic 'owner's manual' for everyone owning a Shih Tzu and also for those who are considering buying a Shih Tzu. What we have done in this book is to give the basic information to help the future owner of a Shih Tzu look after his or her pet responsibly. Too many people still buy a pet before really understanding what they're about to get into.

This book goes into the broad history of the Shih Tzu, the breed standard and some pros and cons of buying a Shih Tzu. You will also find essential information on feeding, initial training and an introduction to reproduction. Finally we pay attention to day-by-day care, health and some breed-specific ailments.

Based on this information, you can buy a Shih Tzu, having thought it through carefully, and keep it as a pet in a responsible manner. A properly brought-up and well-trained dog is more than just a dog. Invest a little extra in a puppy training course or an obedience course. There are also excellent books available that go deeper into certain aspects than is possible here.

About Pets

In general

The Shih Tzu is an eye-catching and charming companion dog of sweet disposition and full of mischief. Its long coat, when left in natural length, requires a considerable amount of grooming if it has to look nice. First and foremost a companion dog, the Shih Tzu thrives on human affection and companionship.

Origin

The origins of the Shih Tzu remain rather mysterious. It is known that the breed is from Tibetan origin, although it is impossible to determin the exact time when this took place. Dogs have always been highly valued in the Tibetan society and religion. Dogs have been bred in monasteries and in palaces, as well as in remote villages. They have enjoyed good treatment and human affection. Due to a close relationship between Tibet and the Chinese Empire, Tibetan dogs found their way to the Imperial Palace in Peking. In this Imperial Palace, the Shih Tzu were kept in big numbers at least since the establisment of the Manchu (Ching) Dynasty in the XVIIth century.

Strict rules were applied to both general care and breeding, which aimed to result in the smallest possible size and the greatest similarity to a miniature lion. Dog breeding in the Palace came to its peak during the reign of Emperor Tao Kung and the Empress Dowager – Tzu Hsi (died 1908). She personally supervised several hundreds of dogs; some of them were classified as the Tibetan strain and were distinctly different from the already established Pekingese. Their heads were longer and the coat was long and shaggy with a slight wave. After the Empress Dowager's death the Imperial kennels were reduced to a large extent and at the time of the Revolution (1924) the Imperial kennels were closed down. Some dogs, however, went to private homes. Several of those so-called "Tibetan Lion Dogs" were eventually exhibited at Peking dog shows. The Breed Club was formed and the breed standard was written in 1933 by the French citizen, Countess D'Anjou.

Meanwhile the first pair of Shih Tzu was brought to Great Britain by Lady Brownrigg upon her returning to her country, which had to become the new homeland for the breed. That original pair, together with dogs brought into Norway by Mrs Kauffmann, formed the foundations of modern breeding outside China.

The British Club was established by Lady Brownrigg, who remained faithtful to the breed for more than thirty years. The Shih Tzu breed started to increase and gained popularity in the sixties and nowadays it is one of the most popular companion dogs worldwide.

Characteristics

Even though the Shih Tzu is a small dog, it is sturdy, tough and mentally stable. It has a lot of self-confidence and it behaves as if it was much bigger than it is. The only purpose of this breed has always been that of a companion and a pet. For that reason this dog is never nervous or shy; it is not supposed to be noisy, either. Apart from the time needed for grooming, it is one of the best house and pet dogs that also are good to be kept with children. Of course, children should be trained to learn that they cannot be too rough with it. The Shih Tzu is kind to other domestic pets and should be kept as a full-time house pet. It needs constant attention and human companionship.

Appearance

Anyone who happens to see a well-groomed Shih Tzu will agree that it is a dog of great beauty. It moves with a smooth, free, ground-covering stride, it carries its head proudly and high, as if it is looking at the world from above. The standard describes this attitude as distinctly arrogant, but

this can be better regarded as being self-confident. Its unique expression comes from the short, broad muzzle, the large eyes and the domed skull. The Shih Tzu is small, but it is sturdily built and heavily boned. Its body is slightly longer than its height, its ribcage is broad, and the tail is curled gaily over the back, well covered with abundant hair that forms a plume. The whole body, including the head, is well covered with long hair. On the head it is neatly tied up to form the so-called "topknot". Although this long coat adds natural beauty to the dog, it can be clipped for your own convenience. The clipped adult dog resembles a big puppy.

UK Kennel Club and its breed standards

What does the UK Kennel Club do?

To say it in their own words: "The Kennel Club is committed to developing and supporting a nation of responsible dog owners. As well as organising events and campaigns to help dog owners meet their responsibilities, the Kennel Club also produces a range of literature to assist the dog owning public."

What is the use of a Breed Standard?

The Kennel Club's answer: "The basis of breed shows is the judging of dogs against the 'Breed Standard', which is the prescribed blueprint of the particular breed of dog. For all licensed breed shows, the Kennel Club Breed Standards must be used for the judging of dogs."

More about the UK Kennel Club Breed Standards: "The Breed Standards are owned by the Kennel Club, and all changes are subject to approval by the Kennel Club General Committee. New Breed Standards, for newly recognised breeds, are drawn up once the breed has become sufficiently established within the UK. Careful research is conducted into the historical background, health and temperament of any new breed before Kennel Club recognition is granted. The Kennel Club currently recognises 196 breeds. Upon recognition, breeds are placed on the Imported Breed Register until they are deemed eligible for transferral to the Breed Register".

A standard provides a guideline for breeders and judges. It is something of an ideal that dogs of each breed must strive to match. With some breeds, dogs are already being bred that match the ideal. Other breeds have a long way to go. There is a list of defects for each breed. These can be serious defects that disqualify the dog, in which case it will be excluded from breeding. Permitted defects are not serious, but do cost points in a show.

The Shih Tzu is listed in the utility group. The Shih Tzu shares this group with miscellaneous dog breeds. These are mainly of a non-sporting origin, such as the Bulldog, Dalmatian, Japanese Akita and Poodle.
Some breeds listed in the utility group are the oldest documented dog breeds in the world and the group is extremely varied. Most breeds were selectively bred for a specific function and do therefore not fit in the sporting and working categories.

The first breed standard

Great Britain 1935
The UK Kennel Club breed standard for the Shih Tzu

General Appearance
Sturdy, abundantly coated dog with distinctly arrogant carriage and chrysanthemum-like face.

Characteristics
Intelligent, active and alert.

Temperament
Friendly and independent.

Head and Skull
Head broad, round, wide between eyes. Shock-headed with hair falling well over eyes. Good beard and whiskers, hair growing upwards on the nose giving a distinctly chrysanthemum-like effect. Muzzle of ample width, square, short, not wrinkled; flat and hairy. Nose black but dark liver in liver or liver marked dogs and about one inch from tip to definite stop. Nose level or slightly tip-tilted. Top of nose leather should be on a line with or slightly below lower eye rim. Wide-open nostrils. Down-pointed nose highly undesirable, as are pinched nostrils. Pigmentation of muzzle as unbroken as possible.

Eyes
Large, dark, round, placed well apart but not prominent. Warm expression. In liver or liver-marked dogs, lighter eye colour permissible. No white of eye showing.

Ears
Large, with long leathers, carried drooping. Set slightly below crown of skull, so heavily coated they appear to blend into hair of neck.

Mouth
Wide, slightly undershot or level. Lips level.

Neck
Well proportioned, nicely arched. Sufficient length to carry head proudly.

Forequarters
Shoulders well laid back. Legs short and muscular with ample bone, as straight as possible, consistent with broad chest being well let down.

Body
Longer between withers and root of tail than height of withers, well coupled and sturdy, chest broad and deep, shoulders firm, back level.

Hindquarters
Legs short and muscular with ample bone. Straight when viewed from the rear. Thighs well rounded and muscular. Legs looking massive on account of wealth of hair.

Feet
Rounded, firm and well padded, appearing big on account of wealth of hair.

Tail
Heavily plumed, carried gaily well over back. Set on high. Height approximately level with that of skull to give a balanced outline.

Gait/Movement
Arrogant, smooth-flowing, front legs reaching well forward, strong rear action and showing full pad.

Coat
Long, dense, not curly, with good undercoat. Slight wave permitted. Strongly recommended that hair on head tied up.

Colour
All colours permissible, white blaze on forehead and white tip to tail highly desirable in parti-colours.

Size
Height at withers not more than 27 cms (101/2 ins), type and breed characteristics of the utmost importance and on no account to be sacrificed to size alone. Weight: 4.5-8 kgs (10-18 lbs). Ideal weight 4.5-7.5 kgs (10-16 lbs).

Faults
Any departure from the foregoing points should be considered a fault and the seriousness with which the fault should be regarded should be in exact proportion to its degree and its effect upon the health and welfare of the dog.

Note
Male animals should have two apparently normal testicles fully descended into the scrotum.

Courtesy of the Kennel Club UK September 2000

Purchase

If, after careful consideration, you have decided to buy a Shih Tzu, there are a number of possibilities. Do you want a puppy or an adult dog? Should it be a male or female?
And, of course, the question arises as to where you should buy the dog. Should you buy it privately or from a reliable breeder? For your own and the animal's sake, a few things should be decided in advance. After all, you want a dog that suits your situation.

Pros and cons of the Shih Tzu

The long coat of this breed needs a lot of care every day. This can be both an advantage and a disadvantage. Some people do not enjoy spending a lot of time grooming their dog, whereas others particularly enjoy making their dog as beautiful as possible. A well cared for Shih Tzu will attract everybody's attention.

The Shih Tzu has an undercoat. This means that they go through a moulting period, and they need a lot of attention when it comes to grooming. An advantage is that these dogs have no problems keeping themselves warm and that they do not need extra protection when it gets cold.

These dogs are very small and they fit into any house. This is, of course, an advantage. They do not need very much exercise, but it is better for them if they build up a good condition. This breed is very focused on its master and it loves to be with him/her as much as possible. They will follow you around all day long. A Shih Tzu becomes approximately twelve years old. Both visitors and the postman are announced with loud barking.

Male or female?

Whether you buy a male or a female is mainly a question of personal preference. Both can grow up to become attractive and well behaved members of the family. And as far as working capacity is concerned, there is no difference between a dog and a bitch.

Males sometimes seem somewhat more self-assured and can display dominant behaviour, trying to play boss over other dogs, especially over other males, and, if they get the chance, over humans too. In the wild the most dominant dog (or wolf) is always the leader of the pack. In many cases this is a male. It is of the utmost importance for a good relationship between dog and master that the dog understands from the outset that you are the leader of the pack. This demands an understanding yet consistent upbringing.

With the Shih Tzu, the difference in character between a male and a female is also not that great. With a Shih Tzu, you also do not need to worry that it will pull too much. You can also teach it to urinate only once or twice each time you take it out on the lead.

When females become fertile, usually between eight and twelve months, they go on heat. This happens twice per year and lasts two to three weeks. This is the fertile period when a female can mate and, especially during the second half of their season, they will try to go out in search of a male. Measures need to be taken to prevent unwanted additions to the family. A male will display more masculine behaviour once he becomes sexually mature. He will make clear to other dogs which territory is his by urinating frequently and in as many places as possible. He's also difficult to confine when there is a bitch in season in the area. However, as far as general care is concerned, there is little difference between male and female.

A puppy test is good for defining what kind of character a young dog will develop. During this test one usually sees that a male dog is more dominant than a female dog. You can often quickly recognise the bossy, the adventurous and the cautious characters. So visit the litter a couple of times early

on. Try to choose a puppy that suits your own personality. A dominant dog, for instance, needs a strong hand. It will often try to see how far it can go. You must regularly make it clear who is the boss, and that it must obey all the members of the family.

Puppy or adult dog?

After you have made the decision for a male or female, the next question comes up. Should it be a puppy or an adult dog? Your household circumstances usually play a major role here.

Of course, it is great having a sweet little puppy in the house, but bringing up a young dog requires a lot of time. In the first year of its life it learns more than during the rest of its life. This is the period when the foundations are laid for elementary matters such as house-training, obedience and social behaviour. You should reckon on, especially in the first few months, having to devote a lot of time to caring for your puppy and bringing it up. You would not need so much time with a grown dog. It has already been brought up, but this does not mean it will not need correcting from time to time.

A puppy will no doubt leave a trail of destruction in its wake for the first few months. With a little bad luck, this will cost you a number of rolls of wallpaper, some good shoes and a few socks. In the worst case you will be left with some chewed furniture. Some puppies even manage to tear curtains from their rails. With good upbringing this 'vandalism' will quickly disappear, but you will not have to worry about this if you get an older dog.

The greatest advantage of a puppy, of course, is that you can bring it up your own way. The upbringing a dog gets or does not get is a major influence on its whole character. Finally, financial aspects may play a role in your choice.
A puppy is generally much more expensive than an adult dog, not only in purchase price but also in maintenance.
A puppy needs to go to the veterinarian more often for the necessary vaccinations and check-ups.

Overall, bringing up a puppy requires a good deal of energy, time and money, but you have its upbringing in your own hands. An adult dog requires less money and time, but its character is already formed. You should also try to find out about the background of an adult dog. Its previous owner may have formed its character in somewhat less positive ways.

Two dogs?

Having two or more dogs in the house is not just nice for us, but also for the animals themselves. Dogs get a lot of pleasure from each others' company. After all, they are pack animals. If you are sure that you want two young dogs, it is best not to buy them at the same time. Bringing a dog up and establishing the bond between dog and master takes time and you need to give a lot of attention to the dog in this phase. Having two puppies in the house means you have to divide your attention. Apart from that, there is a chance that they will focus on one another rather than on their master.

Buy the second pup when the first is (almost) an adult. Two adult dogs can happily be brought into the household together. Luckily, Shih Tzu do not tend to be fighters and they enjoy the company of other dogs of their own breed. Taking in a puppy when the first dog is somewhat older often has a positive effect on the older dog. The influence of the puppy seems almost to give it a second childhood. The older dog, if it has been well brought up, can help with the upbringing of the puppy. Young dogs like to imitate the behaviour of their elders. Do not forget to give both dogs the same amount of attention. Take the puppy out alone at least once per day during the first eighteen months. Ensure both dogs get enough peace and quiet.

The combination of a male and female needs special attention with any breed and with the Shih Tzu too. If you do not plan to breed with your dogs, you must take measures to prevent them mating when the bitch is in season. Spaying the bitch or neutering the male are possibilities, but the latter is usually only done on medical advice, or for behavioural reasons. Sterilisation or castration is, of course, a solution, however it is a final one. A sterilised or castrated animal can never reproduce again. A consequence of sterilisation or castration is that this can lead to abundant hair growth, which usually means a thicker, duller and softer coat which is difficult to groom.

The Shih Tzu and children

Dogs and children are a great combination. They can play together and get great pleasure from each other. Moreover, children need to learn how to handle living beings; they develop respect and a sense of responsibility by caring for a dog, or other pets. However sweet a dog is, children must understand that a dog is a living being and not a toy. A dog is not comfortable when it is being messed around with. It can become frightened, timid and even aggressive. So make it clear what a dog likes and what it does not like. With the Shih Tzu, it is important to make sure that the dog does not allow the child too much. Look for ways the child can play with the dog, perhaps a game of hide-and-seek, where the child hides and the dog has to find it. Even a simple tennis ball can give enormous pleasure. Children must learn to leave a dog in peace when it does not want to play any more. The dog must also have its own place where it is not disturbed. Have children help with your dog's care as much as possible. A strong bond will be the result.

A young Shih Tzu with its limitless energy often does not know when to stop, and you must usually pick the moment when the game is over. A cage or an indoor kennel can be useful here, because a dog needs regular periods of rest for its growth.

The arrival of a baby also means changes in the life of a dog. Before the birth you can help get the dog acquainted with the new situation. Let it sniff at the new things in the house and it will quickly accept them. When the baby has arrived, involve the dog as much as possible in day-by-day events, but make sure it gets plenty of attention too. NEVER leave a dog alone with young children. Crawling infants sometimes make unexpected movements, which can easily frighten a dog. Infants are hugely curious, and may try to find out whether the tail is really fastened to the dog, or whether it can get its eyes out, just like it can with its cuddly toys. A dog is a dog and it will defend itself when it feels threatened.

A dog and cats

Despite the fact that their body language is very different, dogs and cats can actually get on a lot better with each other than many people think. For example, a dog lying on its back is submissive. A cat lying on its back is not at all submissive, but makes sure that it has its best weapons of defence, i.e. its claws, at its disposal. However, dogs and cats have one thing in common: they growl when they are angry, and both animals understand this.

As far as nutrients are concerned, dogs and cats must not share each other's food. Dog food may lack high enough levels of taurine, which is essential for cats. Dogs and cats must also not share a food bowl, as a dog will not tolerate another animal sharing its bowl. A persistent kitten might therefore get a serious ticking off from your dog. Playing together is fine, but you must prevent your pets eating together.

Some dogs will love to chase your cat around. You must prohibit this behaviour from the very beginning. The cat also has its rights and the dog will have to learn not to chase everything that moves. You can take your dog to special classes to help deal with this.

Some dogs (this is not a characteristic of any particular breed) love to eat cat faeces (coprophagia). To prevent your

dog eating from the cat litter, place the litter box in another room, where only your cat has access. Or place the litter box between two pieces of furniture in a manner that prevents your dog gaining access.

Where to buy your dog

There are various ways of acquiring a dog. The decision for a puppy or an adult dog will also define for the most part where to buy your dog.

If it has to be a puppy, then you need to find a breeder with a litter. If you chose a popular breed, like the Shih Tzu, there is enough choice. But you may also face the problem that there are so many puppies on sale that have only been bred for profit's sake. You can see how many puppies are for sale by looking in the regional newspaper every Saturday. Some of these dogs have a pedigree, but many do not. These breeders very often do not watch out for breed-specific illnesses, nor for inbreeding or any hereditary breeding faults and defects; puppies are separated from their mother as fast as possible and are thus insufficiently socialised. NEVER buy a puppy that is too young, or whose mother you were not able to see.

Fortunately there are also enough bona-fide breeders of Shih Tzu who have been involved with the breed for many years as serious breeders and exhibitors and who are only too willing to help you get your Shih Tzu. Try to visit a number of breeders before you actually buy your puppy. Check the parent dogs' papers to ensure they were free of Patella Luxation and be sure that the eyes of the parent have been checked for cataract.
Ask if the breeder is prepared to help you after you have bought your puppy, and to help you find solutions for any problems that may come up.

Shopping list
- Collar
- Lead
- ID tag
- Blanket
- Water bowl
- Food bowl
- Poop scoop
- Dry food
- Canned food
- Comb
- Brush
- Toys
- Dog basket
- Indoor kennel

We recommend you buy a Shih Tzu through the breed clubs. Breeders who are members of the association must meet its breeding rules. Any breeder that does not stick to these strict conditions is expelled. Under these rules both parents must be examined for Patella Luxation and both parents must be free from hereditary cataract.

The puppy service of the breeder clubs can help you with addresses for reliable breeders. The breed federation exercises a very strict breeding policy intended to keep the Shih Tzu population healthy and free of congenital defects. It also allows its members to breed only with animals that are registered with The Kennel Club or with foreign clubs recognised by The Kennel Club.

The breed clubs may be able to inform you about available puppies of breeders who are members of the association. They will often publish lists of litters that have been bred according to their guidelines. To be recognised as a breeder by the breed associations, a breeder must fulfil certain requirements. Some breed associations also have a puppy information service, where you can get information about puppies available within the association. They also help to place adult dogs that can no longer be kept by their owners due to personal circumstances (divorce, moving home etc.).

Finally, you must also realise that a pedigree is nothing more or less than evidence of descent. The Kennel Club also awards pedigree certificates to the offspring of parents that suffer from hereditary defects, or that have not been examined for these. A pedigree says nothing about the health of the parents.

Things to watch out for

Buying a puppy is no simple matter. You must pay attention to the following:

- Never buy a puppy on impulse, even if it is love at first sight. A dog is a living being that will need a lot of care and attention over a long period. It is not a toy that you can put away when you are done with it. You choose a dog to be a comrade and companion for many years.
- Take a good look at the mother. Is she calm, nervous, aggressive, well cared for or neglected? The behaviour and condition of the mother is not only a sign of the quality of the breeder, but also of the puppy you are about to buy.
- Avoid buying a puppy whose mother was kept only in a kennel. A young dog needs as many stimuli and experiences as possible during its early months, including family life. It can thus get used to humans, other pets and different sights and sounds. Kennel dogs miss these experiences and have not been sufficiently socialised.

- Always ask to see the papers of the parents vaccination certificates, pedigrees and official reports on health examinations.
- Ask whether the pups have been vaccinated and wormed or not. Puppies must be vaccinated in the 6th, 9th and between the 12th and 14th week. Regular worming is also extremely important. The first worming has to be done when the puppies are 3 weeks old and after that every two weeks.
- Never buy a puppy younger than eight weeks.
- Put any agreement with the breeder in writing. A model agreement is available from the Kennel Club.

Ten golden puppy rules

1. Walk your puppy in doses followed by one hour play, a feed and then three hours sleep.
2. Never let a puppy run endlessly after a ball or a stick.
3. Do not let your puppy romp wildly with large, heavy dogs.
4. Do not let your puppy play on a full stomach.
5. Do not give your puppy anything to drink straight after its food.
6. Do not let your puppy go up and down the stairs in its first year. Also be careful with smooth floors.
7. Never add supplements to ready-made dogfood.
8. Watch you puppy's weight. Being overweight can lead to bone abnormalities.
9. Give your puppy a quiet place to sleep.
10. Pick up your puppy carefully, one hand under its chest and the other hand under its hindquarters.

Travelling

Travelling with a dog is not always pure pleasure. Some dogs love a ride in the car while others need huge efforts to even get them in it. Some dogs suffer from car-sickness their whole life. If you are planning a holiday in far-away places and want to take your dog with you, you should ask yourself whether you are really doing it a favour.

That very first trip

The first trip of a puppy's life is also the most nerve-wrecking. This is the trip from the breeder's to its new home. If possible, pick up your puppy in the early morning. Then it will have the whole day to get used to the new environment. Ask the breeder not to feed your puppy on that day. The young animal will be overwhelmed by all kinds of new experiences. First of all, it goes away from its mother and its littermates; it has to go into a small room (the car) with all its new smells, noises and strange people. So there is a big chance that the puppy will be car-sick this first time, with the annoying consequence that it will remember travelling in the car as an unpleasant experience.

So it is important to make this first trip as pleasant as possible. When picking up a puppy, always take someone with you who can sit on the back seat with the puppy on his or her lap and talk to it calmly. If it is too warm in the car for the puppy, a place on the floor at the feet of your companion is ideal. The pup will lie there relatively quietly and may even take a nap. Ask the breeder for a cloth or something else from the puppies' basket or bed that carries a familiar scent. The puppy can lie on this in the car, and this will also help if it feels lonely during the first nights at home.
If the trip home is a long one, then stop for a break once in a while. Let your puppy roam and sniff around on the lead, offer it a little bit to drink and, if necessary, let it do its business. And take care to lay an old towel in the car. It can happen that the puppy, in its

nervousness, may urinate or be sick. It is also good advice to give a puppy positive experiences with car journeys. Make short trips to nice places where you can walk and play with it. After all, once in a while you will have to take your dog to certain places, such as to the veterinarian or to visit friends or acquaintances.

Taking your Shih Tzu on holiday

When making holiday plans, you also need to think about what you are going to do with your dog during that time. Are you taking it with you, putting it into a boarding kennel or leaving it with friends? In any event there are a number of things you need to do in good time. If you want to take your dog with you, you need to be sure before you leave that your dog will be welcome at your holiday home, and you also need to check what rules there are. If you are going abroad it will need certain vaccinations and a health certificate, which normally needs to be done four weeks before departure. You must also be sure that you have made all the arrangements necessary to bring your dog back home to the UK, without it needing to go into quarantine under the rabies regulations. Your vet can give you the most recent information.

If your trip goes to southern Europe, ask for a treatment against ticks (you can read more about this in the chapter on *parasites*).

Although dog owners usually enjoy taking their dog on holiday, you must seriously ask yourself if the dog is going to enjoy it as well. With its short muzzle and nose, a Shih Tzu certainly does not always feel comfortable in a hot country. Days spent travelling in a car are equally unpleasant for many dogs, and as we already saw, some dogs suffer badly from car-sickness. There are good medicines to prevent this, but they can also have side-effects and it is questionable if you are doing your dog a favour with these medicines. In case you do decide to take your dog with you, make regular stops at safe places during your journey, so that your dog can have a good run.Take plenty of fresh drinking water with you, as well as the food your dog is used to. Never leave your dog in the car when the sun is shining. The temperature can climb fast and this can very quickly become an awful and life-threatening situation for your dog. If you can not avoid it, park the car in the shade as far as possible and leave a window open for a little fresh air. Even if you have taken these precautions, frequently check on your dog and never stay away longer than is strictly necessary.

If you are travelling by plane or ship, make sure in good time that your dog can travel with you and what rules you need to observe. You will need some time to make all the arrangements. Maybe you decide not to take your dog with you, and then you must find a place where your dog can stay.
Arrangements for a place in a boarding kennel need to be made well in advance, and there may be certain vaccinations required, which need to be given at least one month before the stay.

If your dog cannot be accommodated in the homes of relatives or friends, it might be possible to have an acquaintance stay in your house. This also needs to be arranged well in advance, as it might be difficult to find someone who can look after your dog.
Always ensure that your dog can be traced in case it should run away or get lost while you are on holiday. A little tube with your address or a tag with home and holiday address and a mobile telephone number can prevent a lot of problems.

Moving home

Dogs generally become more attached to humans than to the house they live in. Moving home is usually not a problem for them. But it can be useful before moving to let the dog get to know its new home and the area around it.

If you can, leave your dog with relatives or friends or in a boarding kennel on the day of the move. The chance of it running away or getting lost is then practically zero. When your move is complete, you can pick your dog up and let it quietly get familiar with its new home and environment. Give it its own place in the house at once and it will quickly adapt.

During the first week or so, always walk your dog on a lead, because an animal can also get lost in new surroundings. Always take a different route so it quickly gets to know the neighbourhood.

Do not forget to get your new address and phone number engraved on the dog's tag. Send a change of address notice to the institution that has the microchip or tattoo data (in the UK tattooing is not very common). In some communities dogs need to be registered.

Feeding

A dog will actually eat a lot more than just meat. In the wild it would eat its prey complete with skin and fur, including the bones, stomach and intestines with their semi-digested vegetable material. In this way the dog supplements its meat menu with the vitamins and minerals it needs. This is also the basis for feeding a domestic dog.

Basic principles of dog food

In general

Dogs have always been primarily carnivores (meat eaters). A minor part of their daily diet consists of vegetable material or the vegetable-based content of their prey's stomach and intestines. In the past, dogs kept as pets used to be fed the remains of the family dinner.

Nowadays, most dogs are fed a diet of dry food and/or canned food. The diets of our domestic dogs and cats have changed remarkably over the last fifteen years. There has been a clear increase in expertise and the foodstuffs have become increasingly differentiated. To fully understand the effects of foods, it is important to have some understanding of the anatomy and physiology of dogs.

Anatomy and physiology of the dog's digestive tract

Ingested food first passes into the mouth, where it is crunched. Dogs have no lateral movement in their jaws and therefore cannot chew, but during this crunching, the food is divided into smaller bits and moistened with saliva. The dog's saliva does not include digestive enzymes, so true digestion does not yet start in the mouth. After swallowing, the food passes through the oesophagus to the stomach, where it is mixed and kneaded with gastric acid, i.e. one of the digestive juices. The gastric acid breaks down the proteins present in the food and kills off a large number of potentially harmful micro-organisms present in the food.

Once the food pulp has been kneaded through thoroughly and fulfils a number of chemical requirements, the closing muscle (pylorus) of the stomach relaxes and the food passes through into the duodenum. The duodenum is the first part of the small intestine. Here, important digestive juices such as gall and the pancreatic juices are added to the food pulp. The gall juices help with the digestion of fat and the pancreatic juices contain enzymes which help with the digestion of carbohydrates, proteins and fat. Enzymes are substances which are produced by the animal itself and which help with chemical transformation during digestion.

The small intestine must furthermore be differentiated into the jejunum, ileum and caecum (appendix). The wall of the small intestine contains cells which provide the digestive juices. The wall has plenty of folds to provide as large a surface area as possible, where bacteria, which help in the digestive processes, and enzymes find a place to attach to.
The actual digestion occurs in the small intestine and the foodstuffs are cut down into tiny pieces which can be absorbed.

After being absorbed by the cells in the intestines, the nutrients are passed on to the blood, which transports the nutrients to the liver. The liver functions as a sort of traffic agent, which decides what needs to happen to the different nutrients and then sends them to the right place.

The large intestine (colon) follows on from the small intestine. The most important function here is to absorb the water from the food pulp. The intestine ends in the closing muscle (anus) via the rectum.

Food

Food contains many nutrients which can be divided into six important groups: proteins, fats, carbohydrates, minerals, vitamins and water. Life cannot exist without water. Water does not actually contain any extra nutrients, unless it is mineral water, which can be very rich in certain minerals.

Proteins

Proteins look like a pearl necklace, consisting of different amino acids (the pearls). The amount and type of amino acids determines the characteristics of the protein in question. The presence of nitrogen in all amino acids is important for the development of tissue.

Proteins fulfil many functions in the body; they are the most important components of tissue, hormones and enzymes. Furthermore, they fulfil other important roles by maintaining water levels in the body, removing toxins and maintaining a good defence system.
Proteins are found in both vegetable (grains, legumes, yeast) and animal (meat, fish, poultry, eggs) form. An adult dog must have at least (20g protein/1000kcal food) 8% protein in the dry matter of its food (NRC 1985; NRC 2006) to keep up the maintenance level.
In fact, if you want to ensure optimum health, maximum performance and a beautiful appearance, this percentage must be somewhat higher.

The story that protein is bad for dogs has long been proven a myth. This was based on research in rats, but at the end of the 70s, research showed that the kidney metabolism

of dogs is by no means as sensitive as that of rats. Since 1993, we have also known that proteins do not have a detrimental influence on growth.

On the contrary, proteins, together with the right exercise, contribute to healthy muscles, which in turn stabilise the skeleton. This is a very important consideration for such conditions as hip dysplasia, for example.
Plenty of proteins therefore contribute to your dog's health.

A shortage of proteins will lead to anaemia, low resistance to illness, loss of muscle tissue, etc. A shortage of proteins is caused not only by insufficient absorption, but also through increased breaking-down of proteins, which may be caused by many forms of stress (mental or physical strain on the individual animal).
An influence of protein on behaviour is not yet clear.

Fat
The most important function of fats is to provide energy. Besides this, fats also provide unsaturated fatty acids. Fatty acids fulfil important functions in the nervous systems and the skin's metabolism, among other things. Fats in the food are very easily digested by dogs; in general they digest as much as 95 - 98%. Dogs, just as humans, prefer food with a higher fat content, which is why it is often added to dog food to make it 'tastier'.
Fat is also important as it stores some vitamins.

Carbohydrates
Carbohydrates always originate in vegetable material.
Starch and sugar are well-known examples of carbohydrates.

You can differentiate between digestible carbohydrates (starch, simple sugars) and non-digestible carbohydrates (cellulose, pectin), which come from the cell membranes and fibres of plants.
Carbohydrates improve the transport of the food pulp in the intestines by stimulating the membrane of the intestines. This stimulates the peristaltic movement of the intestines. A disadvantage is that they increase the volume of the faeces, as they also hold a lot of water. A good compromise are the fibres which function as such throughout the major part of the intestines, and are then broken down at the last stage by bacteria in the large intestine. The fibres are broken down into substances which partly function as a source of food for the cells of the large intestine. Beet pulp, for example, contains these valuable fibres.

Minerals

Minerals only play a minor role in your dog's diet as far as the amount is concerned, but they are absolutely vital. Because minerals are needed in such small amounts, mistakes are easily made.
Minerals are divided into macro-minerals and micro-minerals or trace elements. Calcium (Ca) and phosphorus (P) are well-known macro-minerals. They fulfil an important role in building up the skeleton and, depending on the physiological phase, must be provided by the food in a fixed relation to each other. As phosphorus is of vegetable origin, it can often not be absorbed from the food, as in this form phosphorus cannot be absorbed by dogs (phytate).
Other important macro-elements include: magnesium (Mg) (skeleton, enzymes), sodium (Na), potassium (K) and chlorine (Cl). Some examples of micro-minerals include: iron (Fe) (blood, oxygen transport), copper (Cu) (creation of pigment, blood), zinc (Zn) (enzymes, skin), manganese (Mn) (enzymes), iodine (I) (thyroid hormone) and selenium (Se) (muscle tissue, anti-oxidant).

Vitamins

Vitamins can be of both vegetable and animal origins. Vitamins are divided into water-soluble and non-water-soluble vitamins. Vitamins are also required only in very small amounts and dogs can produce a number of vitamins themselves. Below, we will list a number of important vitamins and their functions.

Some important functions of vitamins

	function	shortage	excess
vitamin A	fertility, skin and eyes	fertility problems, night blindness	abnormal bone metabolism vitamin K deficiency
vitamin D3	bone metabolism	abnormal bone metabolism	abnormal bone metabolism, kidney malfunction
vitamin E	with Se protection, muscle cells, anti-oxidant	fertility problems, muscle dystrophy	
vitamin K	blood clotting	haemorrhages	
vitamin C	collagen metabolism, resistance, mucous membranes	connective tissue damage, haemorrhages, liver necrosis	
B1 (thimaine)	carbohydrate metabolism, nervous system	anorexia, circulation problems, diarrhoea, atrophic reproductive organs	
B2 (riboflavine)	catalyst, energy production, protein metabolism	anorexia, growth delays, circulation problems	
PP (niacine)	catalyst, resistance, skin and mucous membranes	skin problems, anorexia, diarrhoea	
B3 (pantothene acid)	part of coenzyme A, Krebs-cycle	alopecia, anorexia, diarrhoea	
B6 (pyridoxine)	catalyst protein metabolism	skin problems, haematological problems	
biotine	catalyst fatty acid synthesis	coat and skin problems	
folic acid	catalyst AZ synthesis	haematological and skin problems	
B12 (cyanocobalamine)	catalyst cystine/ methiomine metabolism	anaemia, alopecia, growth problems	

Energy

All organic processes require energy. This energy is needed for the body to function, produce tissue and to maintain body temperature, for example.
The energy required must be provided by food. In principal, dogs eat until they have fulfilled their energy requirements. However, due to causes such as boredom, the feeding regime and tastiness of the food, there are many dogs that eat more than they need and become fat and heavy. It is therefore important to regularly check your dog's condition.
A dog will store energy reserves as fat on the ribcage. On short-haired dogs, you must be able to see the last two ribs, and on long-haired dogs you must be able to feel the ribs.

Start feeding your dog with the amount recommended on the food packaging, check your dog's condition once per week and adapt it as necessary. Increase the amount of food if you feel the ribs too clearly, and decrease the amount if you can no longer feel the ribs easily. Particularly puppies of breeds prone to skeletal growth problems must be somewhat on the thinner side while growing up.

Industrial food

Industrial dog foods can be divided into three categories depending on their moisture content: moist, semi-moist and dry food. Moist foods contain 70 - 85% water. Their high moisture content makes them very tasty for dogs, but they spoil more easily. The quality is more difficult to maintain than with dry food. The transport is also a disadvantage for the environment and for the owner: four times as much volume needs to be transported. This type of food is also relatively expensive.

Semi-moist food is dry enough that it does not have to be packed into cans. There are no real advantages to this type of food. Dogs might accept it somewhat more easily than dry food, but it does spoil quite easily due to its higher moisture content. Due to their increased moisture content, frozen foods may also be added to this category.

Dry foods are the most economical and are also not prone to turning mouldy, which means that they

keep for a comparatively long time. The specific manufacturing process makes it easier to ensure constant high quality levels. Technically speaking, mixers belong to dry food until they have had water added. At this point, they also spoil quite quickly.
If you want to compare different types of food with each other, you will need to look at the dry matter (= product without water) contents and ingredients.

It is very difficult to judge the quality of dog food. The packaging does not provide all the information and may also not contain any quality claims. It is therefore a matter of trust and you might want to request some further information from the manufacturer. The amount of faeces also gives an indication: the more faeces, the lower the food quality. This, however, does not apply to fibre-rich foods, such as diet foods, "light foods", senior foods and diabetic foods.

Food quality
There are a number of important points as regards the quality of dog food: the digestibility, the biological value (degree to which the nutrients can be absorbed into the tissue), the manufacturing process and the circumstances under which the food is kept until consumption.

Different terminology is used to indicate quality levels. At the moment, the product range includes super premium, premium, products for the medium segment and products for the economical segment. The lower the quality, the lower the price per kilogram.
Top quality can only be delivered by manufacturers who have the best raw materials available, who conduct thorough research and who have a technologically advanced manufacturing process.
The first threat to the quality is oxidization of the ingredients. Light, oxygen and warmth are threats to food quality. Anti-oxidants therefore do a good job and the user must also ensure hygienic handling of the food. Good-quality food is packaged in an airtight packaging, which also keeps out the light, it has a batch code and can tell you the best before and the manufacture dates.

Physiological phases

Good feeding must be adapted as well as possible to the physiological phase of the individual dog. After all, the physiological phase it is in determines what a dog needs.
A growing dog must produce a lot more tissue and therefore needs more building blocks than an adult dog.
All these growth processes require a lot of energy, which means that the energy need is also higher. Depending on the size of the dog, it will grow for 7 to 18 or even 24 months.
During the growing period the puppy's digestive system is not fully developed and so can only cope with small volumes of food.
It is therefore important that the food is both energy dense (which allows for a smaller feeding volume) and balanced in nutrients for that age and stage in development.

Puppies from a number of usually larger breeds have an increased risk of bone-related growth problems and must therefore be fed specifically adapted food. It is also important to keep these puppies slim when they are growing.

Reproduction and lactation are highly demanding on the bitch and, considering that she has to produce both offspring and milk, you can imagine that her energy needs increase a lot. From the 6th week of the pregnancy, you will therefore need to adapt the amount you feed.
Energy demands also increase if your dog is very active. If there is a lot of stress on muscle tissue, it will need to be repaired from time to time. There is also increasing 'wear' on the blood, which means that more nutrients are needed to produce plenty of blood cells. If you keep your dog in an outdoor kennel, it might also require more energy, as it will lose warmth more easily and it might be more active due to being kept outdoors.

By having a close look at the needs of dogs in different physiological phases, it is possible to develop a food which fulfils specific requirements under certain circumstances. Obviously, such dog food requires a lot more research and high-quality raw materials, which will be reflected in a somewhat higher price. An adequate dog food will ensure optimum health and resistance and is therefore always worth the asking price.

Besides the physiological phase, the size of the dog also matters. Pedigree dogs, of course, have set size standards and on mongrels the size depends on the parent animals. Research has shown that there are many differences between small and large dogs; both in terms of susceptibility to health problems and in anatomy and physiology. The manufacturers of the best dog foods take these differences into account. To give just a few examples of the physiological differences between large and small dog breeds:

	Small dog	**Difference***	**Large dog**
Growth period	8 months	3	24 months
Range of growth	20x birth weight	5	100x birth weight
Length canine tooth	4-5 mm	3	15-16 mm
Energy needs	132 Kcal/kg BW**	3	45 Kcal/kg BW**
Weight digestive tract	7% BW**	>2	2.8% BW**
Life expectancy	> 12 years	+/- 3	7 years

* Difference = factor ** BW = body weight

Of course, breeds have their specific size requirements, and every breed also has its own characteristics, such as a special coat or even breed-specific conditions. Breed-specific foods are therefore becoming increasingly popular. These foods are based on the special nutritional needs of the breed and some foods also contain substances which help to prevent breed-specific conditions developing.

Over the last few years, increasing attention has been paid to the possible effect of dog food in addressing potential health risks. Certain substances are added to the food, for example to increase the burning of fat (L-carnitine), to prevent diarrhoea in puppies (zeolite), to support the cartilage (glucosamine and chondroitin sulphate), etc.
The right food can therefore make a major contribution to your dog's health.

Important guidelines

In general

Buy food only in an undamaged package and have experts (vet, pet shop owner or breeder) advise you. Buying in bulk might be economical, but make sure that you have a food bin. Put a week's supply in a bucket, for example, and place the rest in a food bin in a dark, cool, place. Always make sure that you use up or throw away the last bit and clean out the bin regularly!

Puppy food

Buy the most suitable food for your puppy. The basis for a healthy adult life is laid in the growth period and food plays an important role here. Feed your puppy special puppy food at least as long as it is still growing in length (6 to 24 months, depending on the breed). If your puppy belongs to a breed which is sensitive to growth problems, feed it food which was specifically developed for puppies of that breed or size to keep the risk of problems developing as small as possible.

Adult dog
Choose the food which best suits your dog and adapt the amount you feed to its condition.

Pregnant dog
The food requirements of the bitch increase from the 6th week of pregnancy. In the past, bitches were often fed puppy food in the last stage of the pregnancy or during lactation. However, with today's range of puppy foods, they might not all be suitable, so get expert advice on how best to feed your pregnant bitch.

Older dog
The food requirements of older dogs change quite a lot. Scientifically speaking, older dogs need more easily digestible food, which stimulates the intestines, a normal protein content with high biological value and some support for the heart, the skeleton and to improve resistance to illness.

Puppies, pregnant bitch and mother

Amount of food during pregnancy and suckling period
To ensure that the weight increase is no more than 20% on large bitches and no more than 30% on small bitches, it is important to keep a close eye on the weight of your pregnant bitch.
The more the weight increases, the higher the risk of problems during the birth. During pregnancy and suckling, the bitch must be fed a correctly composed diet to ensure that her food reserves are not completely exhausted. If she is fed an incorrect diet, the bitch will have far more trouble recovering from this very demanding period.

During pregnancy

A bitch is pregnant for approximately 63 days. Her food needs start to increase at around the 5th or 6th week of pregnancy. About 25% of the foetus develops during the first 6 weeks of the pregnancy; the remaining 75% of the foetus develops from weeks 6 to 9. During the last trimester, your bitch will have a particularly high need for:

Energy: + 50 to 70%

Proteins: + 170 to 180%

Minerals: ++ (calcium, phosphorus)

Vitamins: ++

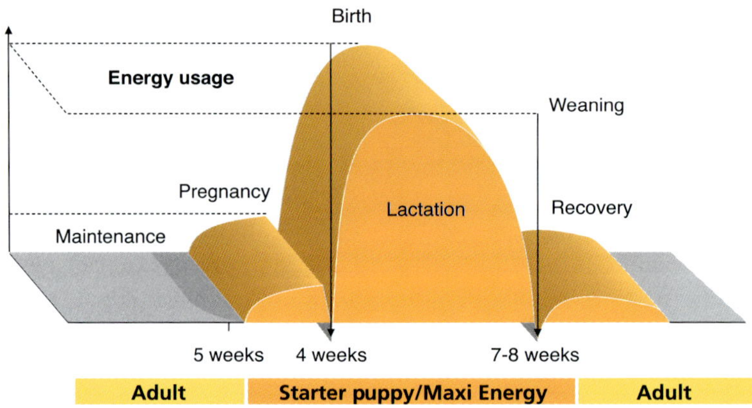

During suckling

The suckling period lasts for 4 to 5 weeks, and the puppies gradually suckle less from the 4th week on. While suckling her offspring, the bitch will have a much higher energy need, as she must also produce the food for them. The mother's milk is very rich in energy and proteins. It is therefore important that the bitch is fed a diet which is high in energy and proteins, and which is very easily digestible. The actual food requirements vary a lot and primarily depend on the size of the litter. The food needs of a suckling bitch may be as follows:
Energy: + 325%
Proteins: + 725%
Minerals: ++++ (calcium, phosphorus)
Vitamins: ++++

To prevent digestive problems, it is advisable to feed the bitch the same food from the last part of the pregnancy until the time that the puppies are fully weaned. The bitch's intestines are particularly sensitive to food changes during this important period. Within 24 hours, a puppy suckles more than twenty times from its mother. The bitch must produce 20 to 25% of a puppy's weight in milk to feed one puppy for one day (so multiply this by the number of puppies in the litter).
The bitch may be fed ad lib during the suckling period, but do keep an eye on her condition.

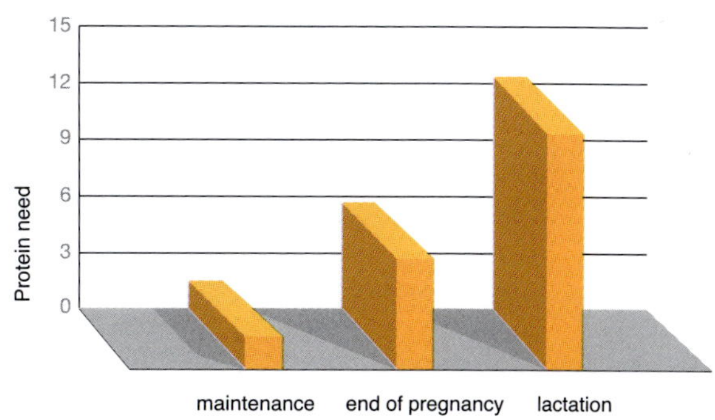

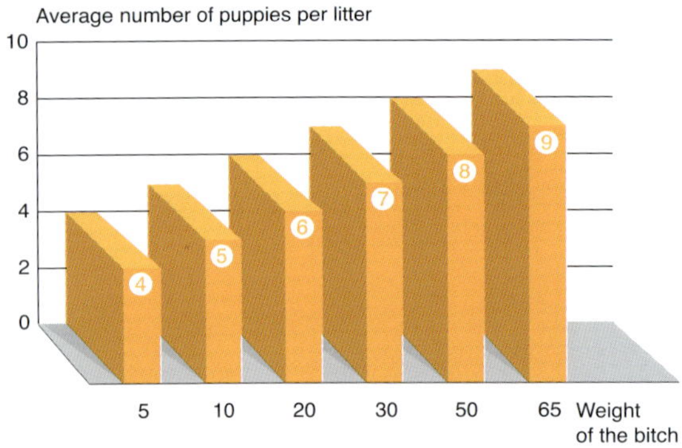

Colostrum is the first milk that the bitch produces after the puppies are born. It is therefore very important that the puppies drink their mother's milk within the first 24 hours after birth. The colostrum contains anti-bodies against infections, which gives the puppies a good start to build up their own solid resistance. If the bitch produces too little milk, you will need to supplement it with special puppy milk.

Puppy during weaning

Right after being born, the puppies depend entirely on their mother's milk as their only food source to stay alive.

It is very important to check your puppies' growth during the first few days by weighing them at exactly the same time every day. Weaning must go very smoothly, so that the puppy and its organs get used to a completely new diet. When the puppy must change from a liquid diet to a solid diet, it is advisable to do this via an extra step.

Energy: + 50 to 70%
Proteins: + 170 to 180%
Minerals: ++ (calcium, phosphorus)
Vitamins: ++

The increasing nutritional needs are best fulfilled by feeding the bitch a specifically composed diet from the fifth or sixth week on. Besides more energy, the bitch also needs more proteins and she needs a concentrated and easily digestible diet, as the uterus pushes onto the stomach during pregnancy, which decreases the stomach volume. The bitch therefore can no longer deal with large amounts of food.

Weaning - an important period

The first step in weaning begins after the third week, when you can start feeding the puppies small amounts of moistened food. During the weaning period, the puppies are quite prone to diarrhoea, which is at least partly due to their limited ability to digest starch. Compared to an adult dog, they only have a 5 - 10% ability to digest starch (see picture). To minimise the risk of diarrhoea and to ensure optimum digestion, feed the puppy a food which is easily digestible and which has a low starch content.

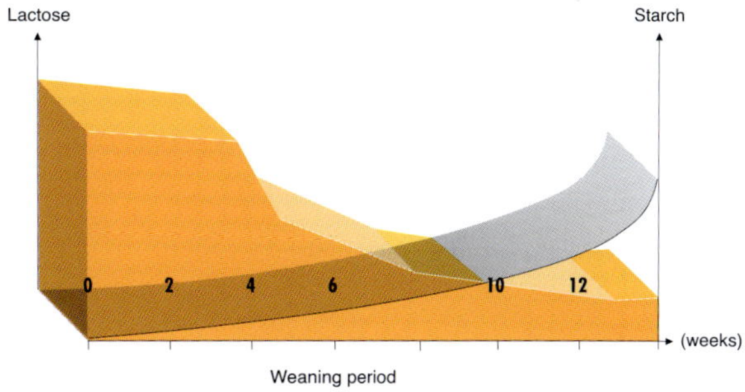

Ready-made foods

It is not easy for a layman to put together a complete menu for a dog, which includes all the necessary proteins, fats, vitamins and minerals in just the right proportions and quantities. Meat alone is certainly not a complete meal for a dog. It contains too little calcium. A calcium deficiency over time will lead to bone defects, and for a fast-growing puppy this can lead to serious skeletal deformities.

If you mix its food yourself, you can easily give your dog too much in terms of vitamins and minerals, which can also be bad for your dog's health. You can avoid these problems by giving it ready-made food of a good brand. These products are well balanced and contain everything your dog needs. Supplements such as vitamin preparations are superfluous. The amount of food your dog needs depends on its weight and activity level. You can find guidelines on the packaging. Split the food into two meals per day if possible and always ensure there is a bowl of fresh drinking water next to its food.

Give your dog the time to digest its food; do not let it outside straight after a meal. A dog should also never play on a full stomach. This can cause bloat (gastric torsion): because of excessive gas content, the stomach becomes overstretched. This can be fatal for your dog.

Because the nutritional needs of a dog depend, among other things, on its age and way of life, there are many different types of dog food available. There are light foods for less active dogs, energy foods for working dogs and senior foods for the older dog.

Canned foods, mixer and dry foods

Ready-made foods available at pet shops or in the supermarket can roughly be split into canned food, mixer and dry food. Whichever form you choose, ensure that it is a complete food with all the necessary ingredients. You can see this on the packaging.

Most dogs love canned food. Although the better brands are composed well, they do have one disadvantage: they are soft. A dog fed only on canned food will not benefit from the gently abrasive effects of dry food and may potentially more quickly develop problems such as plaque, and/or periodontitis. Besides canned food, give your dog hard foods at certain times or a chew especially designed for the oral care of your dog.

Mixer is a food consisting of chunks, dried vegetables and grains. Almost all moisture has been extracted. The advantages of mixer are that it is light and keeps well. You add a certain amount of water and the meal is ready.

A disadvantage is that it must definitely not be fed without water. Without the extra fluid, mixer will absorb the fluids present in the stomach, with serious results. Should your dog manage to get at the bag of mixer or dry chunks and enjoy its contents, give the dog small amounts of water – half a cup – over short time (20 – 30 minutes) intervals.
Dry chunks have also had the moisture extracted but not as much as mixer. The advantage of dry foods is that they are hard, forcing the dog to crunch, removing plaque and massaging the gums.

Dog chew products

Of course, once in a while you want to spoil your dog with something extra. Do not give it bits of cheese or sausage as these contain too much salt and fat. There are various

products available that a dog will find delicious and which are also healthy, especially for its teeth. You will find a large range of varying quality in the pet shop.

The butcher's left-overs

The bones of slaughtered animals have traditionally been given to the dog and dogs are crazy about them, but they are not without risks. Pork and poultry bones are weak. They can splinter and cause serious injury to the intestines. Beef bones are more suitable, but they must first be cooked to kill off dangerous bacteria. Pet shops carry a range of smoked, cooked and dried abattoir left-overs, such as pigs' ears, bull penis, tripe sticks, oxtails, gullet, dried muscle meat, and hoof chews.

Fresh meat

If you do want to give your dog fresh meat occasionally, never give it raw, but always boiled or roasted. Raw or not fully cooked pork or chicken can contain life-threatening organisms. Chicken can be contaminated by the notorious salmonella bacteria, while pork can carry the Aujeszky virus. This disease is incurable and will quickly lead to the death of your pet.

Buffalo or cowhide chews

Dog chews are mostly made of cowhide or buffalo hide. Chews are usually knotted or pressed hide and can come in the form of little shoes, twisted sticks, lollies, balls and various other shapes; nice to look at and a nice change.

Munchy sticks
Munchy sticks are green, yellow, red or brown coloured sticks of various thicknesses. They consist of ground buffalo hide with a number of often undefined additives. Dogs usually love them because these sticks have been dipped in the blood of slaughtered animals. The composition and quality of these between-meal treats is not always clear. Some are fine, but some have been found to contain high levels of cardboard and even paint residues. Choose a product with clearly described ingredients.

Something to drink
A dog can go days without eating if it must, but definitely not without drinking! Make sure it always has a bowl of fresh water available. Food and water bowls of stainless steel are the easiest to keep clean.

Overweight?
Recent investigations have shown that many dogs are overweight. A dog usually gets too fat because of over-feeding and lack of exercise. Medicines or disease are rarely the cause. Dogs that get too fat are often given too much food or too many treats between meals. Gluttony or boredom can also be a cause, and a dog often puts on weight following neutering or spaying. Due to changes in hormone levels, it becomes less active and consumes less energy. Finally, simply too little exercise alone can lead to a dog becoming overweight.

You can use the following rule of thumb to check whether your dog is overweight: you should be able to feel its ribs, but not see them.
If you cannot feel its ribs then your dog is much too fat. Overweight dogs live a passive life; they play too little and tire quickly. They also suffer from all kinds of medical problems (problems with joints and the heart for example). They usually die younger too.

So it is important to make sure your dog does not get too fat. Always follow the guidelines on food packaging. Adapt them if your dog is less active or gets lots of snacks. Try to make sure your dog gets plenty of exercise by playing and running with it as much as you can. If your dog starts to show signs of putting on weight you can switch to a low-calorie food. If it is really too fat and reducing its food quantity does not help, then a special diet is the only solution.

Forbidden food
There is a lot of food which is healthy for people, but that should surely not be given to the dog. Avocados for instance contain the poisonous persin and this can cause an irritated gastro-intestinal tract, but also vomiting, diarrhoea, difficulty in breathing, a build-up of fluid around the heart, and death.
Chocolate is really poison to dogs. The poisonous substance is called theobromine and causes heart palpitation, hallucinations, severe diarrhoea, epileptic attacks, cardiac problems, and death. An average of 30 grams of chocolate per kilo body weight is enough for the dog to be poisoned.
Onions and garlic, although garlic to a lesser degree, contain thiosulfate which can cause anaemia in dogs. Even in case you cook or fry this food, it does not influence the contents, they stay poisonous. Garlic can also cause diarrhoea. Some people think that garlic keeps away the flees from dogs. However this has never been proven.

When dogs eat grapes and/or raisins this can result in death of the dog due to uraemia. Although big individual differences might exist among different dogs, every dog is susceptible for this. The poisonous substance is probably mycotoxin, a poison originating from mould, although this has not yet been proven. For the time being this has not yet been proved. 30 grams of grapes per kilo bodyweight are considered to be poisonous. In case the dog is poisoned it vomits a few hours after eating grapes and three to five days later the symptoms of uraemia can be seen.
In case a dog eats macadamian nuts, this can result in stiffness, fever and stomach-ache. Usually this will disappear after a while. It is also not wise to feed a dog walnuts. Xylitol is a material that substitutes sugar and this material can cause a big decrease in the blood sugar level and it also can cause liver problems. The amount that is found in products that are especially developed for dogs, have no negative influence on the dog.

General nutrional errors

Finally you will find several nutritional matters which are less healthy for human beings as well. This mainly concerns the so-called "nutritional errors".

- As an excuse many say: “In the wild the wolf eats in the same way”, and people feed their domesticated dogs more and more often fresh meat, although our dogs hardly resemble their ancestors anymore. When this is done in the right way, there is nothing wrong with that. However, it is not at all simple to find the right balance and the right composition of the raw materials, which is really necessary to keep the dog healthy in the long term. Especially with young dogs that have to grow, this is of the utmost importance. When the meat is given to the dog while it has not been cooked, the dog runs several risks. This can be parasites such as Toxoplasma, Toxocara, Neospora, Isospora or microbes that can cause severe infections in the body of the dog such as Campylobacter, Salmonella. When people prepare this raw food for their dogs, they also run the risk of being infected. This is called cross-infection.
- In case you feed your dog raw eggs, or eat them regularly yourself, this may cause a lack of vitamin B;
- Food that is too cold, directly from the refrigerator, can cause gastro-intestinal problems.

Care

Good daily care is extremely important for your dog. A well cared-for dog is less likely to become ill. Caring for your dog is not only necessary but also a pleasure. Master and dog are paying each other some attention, and it is an excellent opportunity for a game and a cuddle.

The coat

Caring for your dog's coat involves regular brushing and combing, together with checking for parasites such as fleas and ticks. Shih Tzu a need considerable amount of grooming. How often a dog needs to be brushed and combed depends on the type of its coat. Brushing removes dead hairs and spreads body oil throughout the whole coat. Check your Shih Tzu for tangles behind the ears, in its groin, legs and breech. These tangles are best removed by brushing them out. If a tangle is too big, separate it carefully with your fingers and then comb and brush it out, avoid scissoring as it damages the coat badly. Brush your dog thoroughly twice a week. Never work on a dry coat, but spray it with hairconditioner or even with water before you start brushing. First free up the coat with a stiff brush (rigorously like a massage), layer after layer, and then comb it until all tangles are gone. After that, brush it again with a soft brush to spread the fat and finish it by dividing the coat along the spine. When brushing has been completed, use a rubber band to tie the hair on top of the head into a neat topknot.

Use the right equipment for taking care of the coat. A stiff brush, a soft brush, a medium-fine comb and a fine flea brush (preferably not made of plastic) will do. Combs should not be too sharp. Always brush and comb from the head back towards the tail, following the direction of the hair. Additionally, beard and whiskers should be cleaned, preferably every day. Rinse them with warm water, dry with a cloth and comb afterwards.

Profuse hair between the soles of the feet should be kept short. This is more pleasant for the dog, otherwise it 'slides' on these and collects particles of soil and dirt, making walking unpleasant.

If you get a puppy used to being brushed from an early age, it will enjoy having its coat cared for. A Shih Tzu should be bathed from time to time. Always use a special dog shampoo and make sure it does not get into the dog's eyes or ears. Rinse the suds out thoroughly. A veterinarian can prescribe special medicinal shampoos for some skin problems. Always follow the instructions to the letter. After bathing your Shih Tzu, you should use a hair-dryer and brush until the dog is dry and its coat is free of tangles. Never let the coat of your Shih Tzu dry itself. Make sure your Shih Tzu is completely dry before letting it outdoors again. Even dogs can catch a cold!

Good flea prevention is highly important to avoid skin and coat problems. Fleas must be treated not only on the dog itself but also in its surroundings (see the chapter on *parasites*). Coat problems can also occur due to an allergy to certain food substances. In such cases, a veterinarian can prescribe a hypo-allergenic diet.

If you feel you are unable to cope with the frequent and prolonged grooming sessions, it is better to have your Shih Tzu clipped by a professional dog groom rather than keep it neglected and tangled. It does not mean that a clipped dog does not require grooming, however, it is considerably simpler and easier. Usually a vigorous brush once a week will do.

Teeth

A dog must be able to eat properly to stay in good condition, so it needs healthy teeth. Check its teeth regularly. If you suspect that something is not well, contact your vet. Regular feeds of hard dry food can help keep your dog's teeth clean and healthy. There are special dog chews on the market that help prevent plaque and help keep the animal's breath fresh. What really helps is to brush the teeth of your dog regularly. You can use special toothbrushes for dogs, but a finger wrapped in a small piece of gauze will also do the job. Get your dog used to having its teeth cleaned at an early age and you will have no problems.

You can even teach an older dog to have its teeth cleaned. With a dog chew as a reward it will soon get used to it.

Dental plaque and strong breath

Dental care and a fresh breath are very normal for human beings. However, this is not so natural for our dogs. Although the dog owners get more and more aware of the fact that dental care is important for dogs as well, there still are many dogs that have a strong breath because of dental plaque or tartar.
In the first place, tartar is the cause of gingivitis, which spreads more and more and in the long run this even can cause problems to heart, kidneys and liver. So dental care is no redundant luxury!

Schematic representation of the teeth

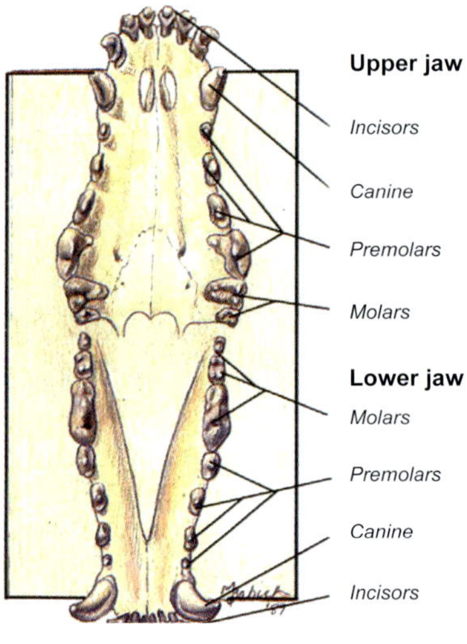

The function of microbes

It is quite normal to have many microbes in the mouth. After every meal a thin layer of food stays behind on the teeth, which is a good culture medium

Left: profile of the teeth
Right: front view of the teeth

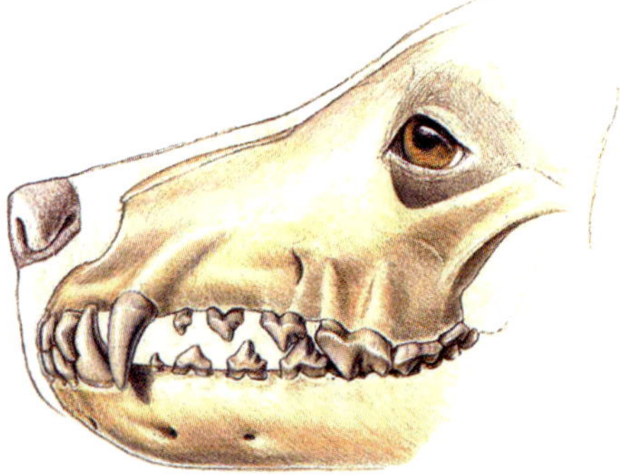

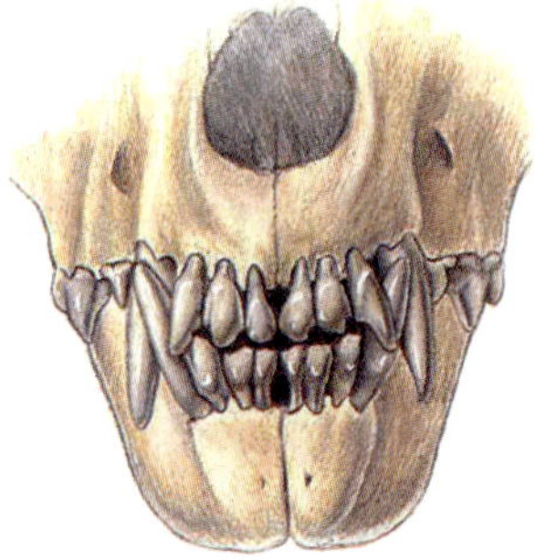

for microbes. All this together is called dental plaque. The degradation products from microbes are acidic and they damage the teeth. As a result of this, gingivitis and paradontitis are formed and as a consequence of that the dog might even lose its teeth. In addition to this it gets more and more difficult to clean the teeth when there is irregular dental care. The fact is, that dental plaque will turn hard as time goes by and then it is called tartar. Tartar can be removed by the veterinarian while the dog will be anaesthetized.

Paradontitis

Dogs fortunately have less problems with cavities. However paradontitis is the most frequent dental problem among dogs. When a dog has this dental problem, the gums, the teeth and the dental alveolus will become affected by microbes in the mouth of the dog.

More than 80% of all adult pets older than three years find themselves in different stages of this dental problem, and have suffered from a strong breath, pain and/or loss of teeth. In the long run, the microbes from the mouth can come into the blood and damage several important organs!

Special feeding

Your veterinarian can prescribe your dog a special diet-food. This food can help your dog in two different ways. First by mechanical cleaning of the teeth through the special form, size and shape of the chunks. By eating this kind of food, the teeth are cleaned and it will prevent that plaque and tartar are built up.

The second way is by adding ingredients that prevent the transformation of plaque into tartar and that also prevent a strong breath.

Additive in drinking water

Nowadays it is possible to add a tasty additive to the drinking water in order to prevent plaque, tartar and strong breath in dogs. This anti-plaque liquid can simply be added to the drinking water of th dog. This product contains the active substances chloro hexidine and xylitol, which restrain the increase of microbes in the mouth and because of that they prevent the building up of plaque. Apart from that, xylitol restrains the building up of tartar and takes care of a fresh breath.

So every time that your dog drinks, the teeth are automatically taken care of. Refresh the drinking water every day, even if there is some water left.

Regular check ups by the veterinarian

Apart from the daily dental care at home, it is to be advised to have a regular check up by the veterinarian. Gingivitis and other dental problems can be found in time. Dogs can hide their dental problems very well! Your veterinarian will clean the teeth of your pet in a very professional way and he also has the right dental care products.

Nails

On a dog that regularly walks on hard surfaces, the nails usually grind themselves down. In this case there is no need to clip its nails. But it would not do any harm to check their length now and again, especially on Shih Tzu that do not get out on the street very often. Using a piece of paper, you can easily see whether its nails are too long. If you can push the paper between the nail and the ground when the dog is standing, then the nail has the right length.

Nails that are too long can bother a dog. It can injure itself when scratching, so they must be kept trimmed. You can buy special nail clippers in pet shops. Be careful not to clip back too far as you could cut into the quick, which can bleed profusely. If you feel unsure, have this important task done by a vet or an animal groomer.

Special attention is needed for the dewclaw, this being the nail on the inside of the hind leg. Clip this nail back regularly, otherwise it can get caught and become damaged.

Eyes

A dog's eyes should be cleaned regularly. Discharge gets into the corners of the eye. You can easily remove it by wiping it downward with your thumb. If you do not like doing that, use a piece of tissue or toilet paper.

Cross-sectional view of the eye

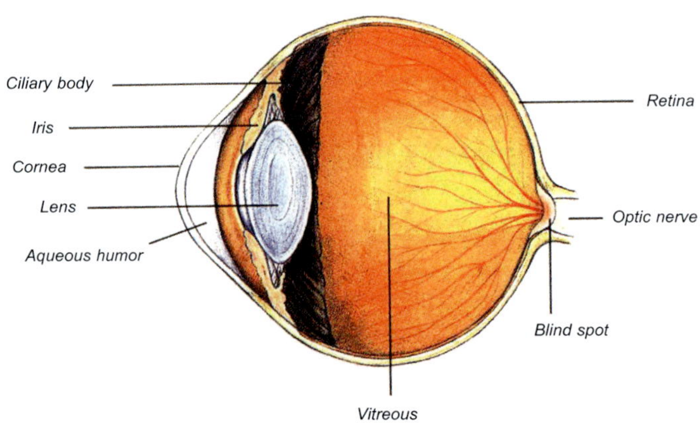

Keeping your dog's eyes clean will take only a few seconds a day, so do it every day. If the discharge becomes yellow this could point to an irritation or infection. When the eyelids are red, this is a sign of an infection which is best taken care of by your veterinarian. The eye drops or ointment that he prescribes will quickly solve this problem.

Ears

The ears are often forgotten when caring for dogs. They must be checked at least once a week. If the ears of your dog are very dirty or show too much wax, you must clean them. This should be done preferably with a clean cotton cloth, moistened with lukewarm water or baby oil. Cotton wool is not suitable due to the fluff it can leave behind.

If hairs inside the ears cause problems, then it is better to remove them. Carefully pull them out by using your thumb and index finger.

NEVER enter the ear canal with an object. If you neglect cleaning your dog's ears there is a substantial risk of infection. A dog that is constantly scratching at its ears might be suffering from dirty ears, an ear infection or ear mites, making a visit to the vet essential.

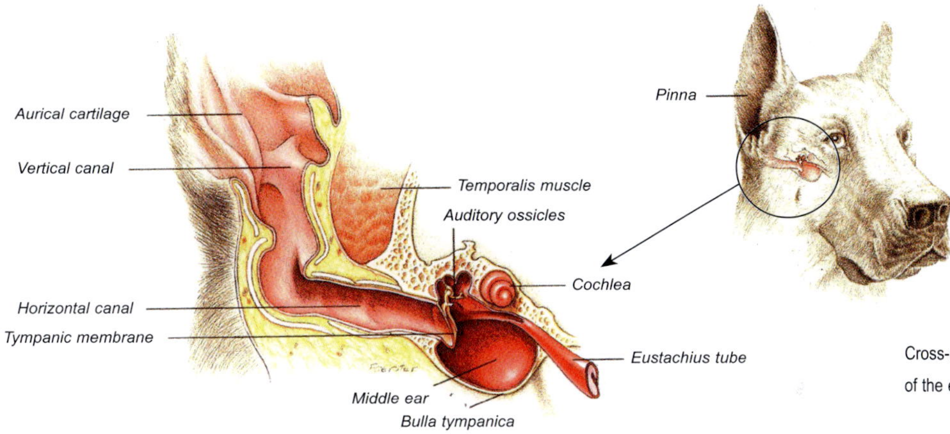

Cross-sectional view of the ear

Anal glands

When a dog sits on its bum and tries to shuffle forward by using only its forelegs (called scooting), then you can be sure that its anal glands are bothering it. The anal sacs of the dog can be found on the left and right side of its anus. In case these sacs are full they start itching and cause pain to the dogs. The dog tries to bite them and if you do not notice it immediately, your dog will bite them completely open. You can prevent this, by squeezing them out. However, if you do not know how to do this, please go to a veterinarian to solve this problem. You can also visit a professional groom.

Rearing

It is very important that your dog is well brought up and obedient. This not only makes it more fun for you to be with your dog, but it also makes it more pleasant for other people.
A puppy can learn in a playful manner what it must and must not do.
Praise and consistency are two very important tools when bringing up a dog.
When you reward your puppy for good behaviour with your voice, a pat or something tasty, it will soon learn to be obedient. A puppy course can be very helpful here.
When dealing with your dog, it is also useful to know something about the life of dogs, i.e. wolves, in the wild.

In the wild, wolves, the ancestors of our dogs, live in packs. They are therefore used to living in a group. Our domestic dogs view their families as their packs. In fact, our dogs see us as dogs, too. Every pack has a hierarchy. This means that there is one boss, the alpha animal, and all the other animals are ranked according to importance, right to the lowest position, the omega animal. There is a constant battle for the alpha spot in the pack. When you take a dog into your home, it is therefore very important to make it clear where its place is in the family. This is simply done by following twelve rules. In this chapter, we deal with the 'rules of the pack', what they are, how you can apply them and what you can do and what you should not do.

The rules of the pack

Rule 1

The Alpha dog sleeps where it wants and no-one is to approach it.

An animal high up in the hierarchy can choose its own place to rest. This place is always respected by the animals lower in the hierarchy. If an inferior animal comes close to a superior animal which is resting, the latter will growl to make it clear that the inferior animal must not approach.

If the inferior animal approaches anyway, there is a real risk that the superior animal will bite. This rule not only applies to resting and sleeping. The superior animal always has access to places which are prohibited to the inferior animal.

The alpha animal is therefore not always the 'official' pack leader; it is the animal highest in the hierarchy present at that moment.

Advice:

- Never let your dog sleep on your bed.
- The bedroom should actually be entirely forbidden territory for your dog.
- You can also prohibit access to other parts of the house. This makes it clear to the dog that you are higher in the hierarchy.
- If your dog lies on a chair which you want to sit on, simply sit down without saying anything. If necessary, sit on your dog.

Don't

- Never try to take away your dog's safe place.
- Never let your dog take away your place.
- Never let your dog refuse people access to certain places.

Rule 2

The alpha male has the highest position.

In a pack of dogs, you can often see that the pack leader lies somewhat higher than the rest of the pack, as if he wants to have a good overview over the pack. The alpha male thus demonstrates his high position.

Domestic dogs also often want to lie on a somewhat higher place and they might try to climb onto the headrest of your sofa in an attempt to demonstrate that they have a high position. Dogs which are lower down in the hierarchy would never dare to demonstrate such behaviour. Dogs demonstrate what position they hold within the pack not just by lying on a higher place, but also with their general attitude.

Advice

- When you notice that your dog wants to lie on a higher position while you are present, do not allow it.

- If, for example, you are sitting on the stairs and your dog comes to sit with you, make sure that it does not sit on a higher step than you do.

Don't

- Never let your dog crawl onto your lap without permission.
- Never pick up your dog to a higher position in the presence of another dog (or human), as this will give your dog an artificial and undeserved higher position.

Rule 3

The alpha male eats first. The others get the left-overs, unless the alpha decides to keep everything for himself.

When the pack has caught a large prey, it is not necessarily divided up democratically. The alpha animal always eats first, possibly together with the alpha bitch at most. The rest of the pack must wait until the leader has finished.

The alpha male will decide when the rest of the pack gets its food. He might also decide that the others do not get anything at all. In this case, he simply puts the remains of the prey somewhere else and moves away. In fact, the alpha animal challenges the inferior animals to take the food. If an inferior animal dares to approach the food, the alpha animal will growl loudly and bite the inferior animal in the neck to correct it, or grab the food away from it to display its higher position.

Advice

- Prepare your dog's food and place it out of reach. Then you go and have dinner first. Only feed your dog when the whole family has finished. Preferably, first give the 'stay' command and then allow your dog to approach its food.

- Place toys on the floor close to your dog. When it wants to take the toy, you grab it away. Repeat this a few times. Your dog will soon stop trying to take the toy. This is the moment when your dog acknowledges your superiority.

Don't

- Never feed your dog anything while the family is having dinner. This gives the dog the same position in the hierarchy as the members of the family.
- Be careful with food envy! Never take food away from your dog and stay away from its food bowl when it is eating.

Food envy

Many dogs refuse to give up things they carry in their mouth (food, toys). If you do try to take these things from your dog, it will growl. We can often see the same behaviour in dogs that are eating. When you approach your dog's bowl, it will growl. This behaviour is called 'food envy'.

Rule 4

Playing, not fighting, is the way to establish hierarchy.

A dog can determine and confirm hierarchical positions during play. For young dogs, in particular, playing is also a way to learn to live in a group, and to slowly find out which position they will have within the pack.

Our pet dogs no longer live according to the harsh laws of nature. This allows them to remain playful to an old age. The only reason for dogs to live in a pack is because this

increases their chances of success when hunting.
If they would constantly fight to determine or confirm their position in the hierarchy, there would be a lot of casualties and an injured animal is no help when hunting. We therefore more often see dogs play than fight to establish the hierarchy. After all, their life partly depends on the health of the others in the pack.
When two strange dogs walk past each other, they will sometimes have a go at each other. As they are not members of the same pack, this has nothing to do with establishing a hierarchy, but with protecting their territory.

Territory
The territory is the domain of the pack. This territory may be several kilometres across and is divided into three different 'sectors'. In the outer circle of the territory, pack members will make it clear to intruders that they must stay out. If an intruder manages to get into the middle circle, the pack will attack him. However, he will be given the chance to escape during this attack. The innermost circle is the centre of the pack. The puppies stay there and the entire pack retreats to this sector to rest. Defending this place is a matter of life and death. If we look at how closely humans live to each other in the Western world, it is not surprising that dogs have so many territorial conflicts. A dog will, after all, not be satisfied with its own garden. Its territory is much bigger. The garden is simply the centre of the territory. The rest is outside your garden fence. This means that the territories of dogs which live closely together overlap each other. Even when walking a dog on the lead, it still has a territory. It is a mobile territory, and the dog sees itself as the centre. It is therefore not surprising that two dogs often have a go at each other when taken out for a walk. After all, the centre of the territory must be defended fanatically.

Advice
- Always keep games under control: you determine the course of a game, not your dog.
- When you are playing with your dog, you must be aware that it constantly tries to get over you in the hierarchy. Therefore constantly pay attention to this rule.
  If you think that your dog is trying to dominate the game, stop immediately and ignore it completely for a while.

Don't

- Never let your dog dominate retrieve or tug-of-war games.
- Never let your dog determine how or what you are going to play. That is your decision.

Rule 5

The alpha wins each and every game.

When dogs are playing, you can see that a superior animal will always assume a higher position than an inferior animal. The superior animal will decide when the game is over and it will always win.

Advice

Make sure that you always win the last game when playing with your dog. It is possible to let your dog win a game once in a while, but you must dominate the major part of it. How many games your dog is allowed to win depends on the hierarchical relationship between you and your dog. A dominant dog should never be allowed to win.
A submissive dog can be allowed to feel like a winner once in a while.

Don't

- Never let your dog win the last game.
- Never finish a retrieve game by throwing the object. The dog will pick up the object and therefore in fact be the winner of the game. A tug-of-war game with a rope must not be finished by letting go of the rope and giving it to the dog. Take the rope and put it away.

Rule 6

Each pack member makes place for the highest in rank.

If a superior animal goes somewhere, all the inferior animals will move out of its way. The superior animal will go in a straight line, without swerving, to the place it wants to go. No other dog will stand in its way. Only inferior animals will move aside.

Don't

- If your dog is coming towards you and wants to move past you, do not move aside.
- Never swerve around your dog if you want to go past it. And do not step over it, even when it is asleep.

Rule 7

The highest in the hierarchy will always go through a narrow passageway first

A narrow passageway is a very wide term in this context. It is not only a doorway or a gate, but it can also be the alleyway between two houses, the space between parked cars or even a forest path.

The clearest example for this rule is a pack of hunting dogs. When these dogs are let out of their kennels, it is always the animal highest in the hierarchy which exits first. Dogs often run ahead when out on a walk. They do this to confirm their higher position in comparison to their owner.

Advice

- Open a door a little. If your dog wants to go through, close it. Be very careful that your dog's nose does not get caught, however! Repeat this until your dog no longer attempts to go through the door. Then go through the door yourself and let your dog follow you.
- Sometimes your dog will try to go ahead of you through a passageway, which cannot be closed with a door or gate. In this case, keep your dog on a four to five metre long lead. Walk towards the passageway. If your dog wants to go ahead, turn around and walk away from the passageway. If your dog does not follow straight away, it will get a sudden pull when the lead tightens. It should now follow you. Repeat these steps until your dog no longer shows the intention of going through the passageway first.

Don't

- You must never try to physically prevent a dog from going through a passageway first. There is no point in forcing your dog physically to accept you as a leader. If you try to stop your dog in such a manner, it will soon learn that it simply has to be faster than you. This way, the dog tries to prevent you stopping it.
- Never let your dog pull on the lead when walking it.

Rule 8

Each pack member pays respect to the alpha male every day.

All dogs in a pack confirm their submissive position every day by consistently applying the rules of the pack. They devote most of their time to the alpha dog, which they honour. This becomes clear in their greetings, for example. First the highest in the hierarchy is greeted, and then the other members according to their status. Everything that happens in a pack reflects the movement from top to bottom. Inferior animals always respect superior animals.

Advice

- Respect all the rules of the pack every day.
- Always respect the hierarchy.
- Always show respect for those superior (for children, this is the parents).

- When eating, when wiping your feet after a walk or when going through a passageway, make sure that you always come first and that your dog always comes last.
- Always greet the highest members of the hierarchy first, and the lower members after that. This means that a dog must be greeted last.

Don't

- It is absolutely wrong to act against the hierarchy. According to the rules of the pack, a superior animal must never let an inferior animal have an advantage.
  It is therefore very confusing for your dog, if, for example, you greet it before you greet the other members of the family.

Rule 9

The alpha dog decides what is best.

The pack leader decides everything that goes on within a pack. He decides when to sleep, when to hunt, when to play, when to eat, etc. No other dog within the pack will make decisions which contradict those of the leader.

Advice

- As the boss, you make all the decisions for your dog within the human/dog pack. You decide when your dog is allowed to go for a walk, to eat, play and sleep.

Don't

- Never let your dog decide. Therefore do not follow its demand (begging) to go for a walk or to play with it. You alone decide when you do anything with your dog.

Rule 10

An inferior member of the pack pays attention to the alpha.

A superior animal never approaches an inferior animal, unless it wants to reprimand it. An inferior animal always approaches a superior animal, and assumes a submissive posture (head low, ears back, tail low). This is called active submission. A superior animal may approach an inferior animal to reprimand it. In this case, the superior animal will assume a superior posture (dominance).

Active submission

Inferior dogs sometimes approach superior dogs. In this case, they assume a low posture: the ears are pinned back, the tail is carried low and the body is generally held somewhat lower towards the ground. When an inferior animal reaches the superior animal, it will lick the corners of its mouth. This is a social

gesture which dogs inherited from their ancestors. With this gesture, the inferior dog confirms the superior dog in its status. We call this active submission: the inferior dog initiates the submission.

Passive submission

In the case of passive submission, the inferior animal also assumes a low posture. The only difference is that this time the superior animal initiates the submission. When it approaches the inferior animal with a superior posture, the inferior animal will react immediately and assume an inferior posture. If it does not do this, it will be reprimanded by the superior animal.

Advice

- Always make your dog approach you.
- Regularly play chase games, where your dog must follow you.
- Only ever approach your dog when you need to reprimand it.

Don't

- Never approach your dog. Particularly not when it is lying in its safe place. The dog wants to have some peace and quiet here. When approaching your dog, you are moving for it and a superior animal never moves for an inferior animal!

Rule 11

Only the alpha animal has the right to ignore.

A superior animal will often ignore the inferior animal when it passes by. An inferior animal would never dare to ignore a superior dog in such a way, it would be punished immediately. In general, a pack leader will usually ignore the lowest members of the pack.

It is also not his job to watch over the entire pack, as this would require far too much energy. Every member of the pack therefore needs to pay attention to the alpha animal. The group thus stays together: where the alpha animal leads, the rest follows.

Advice

- Regularly ignore your dog when passing by. This shows it that you are still higher up in the hierarchy.
- When your dog is importunately demanding your attention or jumping up at you, it is best to ignore it completely. Ignoring it is punishment for your dog. Dogs would rather have negative attention than no attention at all. If you shout at your dog for jumping up at you, you are actually paying attention to it, which is exactly what it wants.

Don't

- Never let your dog ignore you. If necessary, demand its attention or motivate it so that it becomes interested in you again.

Rule 12

A superior animal has the right to allow privileges.

Both with humans and with dogs, we often see that someone who is high up in the hierarchy often deals out privileges to the ones directly below. The lower animal can in turn hand out privileges to the one below it. An animal will never hand out more privileges than it received.

This means that the lowest animal in the hierarchy will have the least privileges of all. Privileges which have been handed out can also be withdrawn. If an animal does not behave exceptionally well, it could easily lose all its privileges.

Advice

- Once you have established the hierarchy within your human/dog pack with the help of the above rules, you can give your dog some privileges. In other words: you may decide to apply some of the rules less strictly. You need to realize that such privileges allow your dog to move a little closer to the rest of the family in terms of hierarchy. Therefore never give your dog too much freedom. Make sure that there is still enough distance in the hierarchy between your dog and the rest of the family.
- You may hand out privileges, but you do not have to!

Don't

- Never allow a dog privileges that are not far enough below those of all the other members of the pack. It will soon take advantage.

(Dis)obedience

A dog that does not want to obey you is not just a problem for you, but also for your surroundings. It is therefore important to avoid unwanted behaviour. In fact, this is what training your dog is all about, so get started early. 'Start them young!' applies to dogs too. An untrained dog is not just a nuisance, but can also cause dangerous situations by running into the road, chasing joggers or jumping at people.
A dog must be trained out of this undesirable behaviour as quickly as possible. The longer you let it go on, the more difficult it will become to correct it. The best thing to do is to attend a special obedience course. This can help to correct the dog's behaviour, as well as helping the owner to learn how to handle undesirable behaviour at home. A dog must not only obey its master during training, but everywhere and at any time.

Always be consistent when training good behaviour and correcting annoying behaviour. Reward the dog for good behaviour and never punish it after the event for any wrongdoing. This means: If your dog finally comes after you have been calling it a long time, then reward it. If you are angry because you had to wait so long, it may feel it is actually being punished for coming. It will probably not obey at all the next time for fear of punishment.

Try to take no notice of undesirable behaviour. Your dog will perceive your reaction (even a negative one) as a reward for this behaviour. If you need to correct the dog, then do this immediately. Use your voice or grip it by the scruff of its neck and push it to the ground. This is the way a mother dog calls her pups to order. Rewards for good behaviour are, by far, preferable to punishment; they always get a better result.

House-training

The very first training and one of the most important that a dog needs is house-training. The basis for good house-training is keeping a

good eye on your puppy. If you pay attention, you will notice that it always sniffs or turns around the same place before doing its business there. Pick it up gently and place it outside, always at the same place. Reward it abundantly if it does its business there.
Always put a puppy out at the same times: In the morning as soon as it is awake, before and after meals, every time it has been asleep or has been playing, and in the evenings before bedtime. It will quickly learn the meaning, especially if it is rewarded with a dog biscuit for a successful attempt. Let it relieve itself before playing with it, otherwise it will forget to do so and you will not reach your goal.

Of course, it is not always possible to go out after every snack or snooze.
Lay newspapers at different spots in the house. Whenever the pup needs to do its business, place it on a newspaper. After some time it will start to look for a place itself. Then start to reduce the number of newspapers until there is just one left, at the front or back door. The puppy will learn to go to the door if it needs to relieve itself. Then you put it on the lead and go out with it. Finally you can remove the last newspaper. Your puppy is now house-trained.

One thing that certainly will not work is punishing an accident after the event. A dog whose nose is rubbed in its urine or its stool will not understand that at all. It will only get frightened of you. Rewarding works much better than punishment. An indoor kennel or cage can be a good tool to help in house-training.

A puppy will not foul its own spot, so an indoor kennel can be a good solution for the night, or during periods during the day when you cannot watch it.
An indoor kennel must not become a prison where the dog is locked up day and night.

First exercises

To get the right result it is important to be clear and consistent during training. Commands should be short and clear, like 'Lie down!' or 'Stay there!'. Commands should always be in the same tone and must be clearly different from one-another.

Be consistent once you have chosen the commands. If you want the dog to lie down, it is no use using 'Lie down!' once and 'Lay!' the next time. Once the dog has understood the intention, it should only be necessary to give a command once, clearly and in a certain tone. Repeating a command actually makes your dog disobedient. If it does not react immediately, make a disapproving sound while walking towards it. Shouting usually does not have the desired result. Dogs have exceptional hearing, much better than a human's. Commands should be given in a quiet and preferably soft tone. Keep raising your voice for exceptional situations.

The basic commands for an obedient dog are those for *sit, lie down, come* and *stay*. But a puppy should first learn its name. Use it as much as possible from the first day on, followed by a friendly 'Here'. Reward it with your voice and a pat when it comes to you. Your puppy will quickly recognise the intention and has now learned its first command in a playful manner. Do not appear too strict towards a young puppy; do not always punish it immediately if it does not always react in the right way. When you call your puppy to you in this way, have it come right to you.

You can teach a pup to sit by holding a piece of dog biscuit above its nose and then slowly moving it backwards. The puppy's head will also move backwards until its hind legs slowly go down. At that moment you say 'Sit!'. Use your free hand to gently push the hindquarters down. After a few attempts, it will quickly understand this nice game. Use the 'Sit!' command before you give your dog its food, put it on the lead or before it is allowed to cross the street.

Teaching the command to get the dog to lie down is similar. Instead of moving the piece of dog biscuit backwards, move it down vertically until your hand reaches the ground and then forwards. The dog will also move its forepaws forwards and lie down on its own. Again, help it with your free hand. Then say 'Lie down!' or 'Lay!'. Lying down is useful when you want a dog to be quiet.
Two people are needed for the 'Come!' command. One holds the dog back while the other runs away. After about fifteen metres, he or she stops and enthusiastically calls 'Come!'. The other person now lets the dog go, and it should obey the command at once. Again you reward it abundantly. The 'Come!' command is useful in many situations and good for safety too.

A dog learns to stay from the sitting or lying position. While it is sitting or lying down, you call the command 'Stay!' and then step back one step. If the dog moves with you, quietly put it back in position, without displaying anger. If you do react angrily, you are actually

punishing it for coming, and you'll only confuse your dog. It cannot understand that coming is rewarded one time, and punished another. Once the dog stays nicely reward it abundantly. Do not let it lay more than a few seconds in the beginning. Once it understands what is expected, you can make the time longer, and increase the distance between you and the dog at the same time. The 'stay' command is useful, for example, when getting out of the car.

Courses

Because it is important that a Shih Tzu is brought up properly, we recommend that you attend an obedience course with your dog. Obedience courses to help you bring up your dog are available across the country.
These courses are not just informative, but also fun for dog and master.

With a puppy, you can begin with a puppy course. This is designed to provide the basic training. A puppy that has attended such a course has learned about all kinds of things that it will confront in later life: other dogs, humans, traffic and what these mean.
The puppy will also learn obedience and to follow a number of basic commands. Apart from all that, attention will be given to important subjects such as brushing, being alone, travelling in a car, and doing its business on the right places.

The next step after a puppy course is a course for young dogs. This course repeats the basic exercises and ensures that the growing dog does not get into bad habits. After this, the dog can move on to an obedience course for full-grown dogs. For more information on where to find courses in your area, contact your local kennel club. You can get the address from The Kennel Club of Great Britain in London. In some areas, the RSPCA organises obedience classes and your local branch may be able to give you information.

Play and toys

There are various ways to play with your dog. You can romp and run with it, but also play a number of games, such as retrieving, tug-of-war, hide-and-seek and catch. Shih Tzu love this kind of games. A tennis ball is ideal for retrieving; and you can play tug-of-war with an old sock or a special tugging rope. Play tug-of-war only when your dog is at least one year old. A puppy must first get its second teeth and then they need several months to strengthen. If you start too young, there is a real chance of your dog's teeth becoming deformed. You can use almost anything for a game of hide-and-seek. A frisbee is ideal for catching games. Never use too small a ball for games. It can easily get lodged into the dog's throat.

Play is extremely important. Not only does it strengthen the bond between dog and master, but it is also healthy for both. Make sure that you are the one that ends the game. Only stop when the dog has brought back the ball or frisbee, and make sure you always win the tug-of-war. This confirms your dominant position in the hierarchy. Use the toys only during play so that the dog does not forget their significance. When choosing a special dog toy, remember that dogs are hardly careful with them. So always buy toys of good quality that a dog cannot easily destroy.

Be very careful with sticks and twigs. The latter, particularly, can easily splinter. A splinter of wood in your dog's throat or intestines can cause awful problems. Throwing sticks or twigs can also be dangerous. If they stick into the ground a dog can easily run into them with an open mouth.

For people who want to do more, there are various other sporting alternatives such as behaviour, obedience, and road safety.

Aggression

Shih Tzu should never appear aggressive. But even they can sometimes be quite bossy and difficult with other animals or people, for that reason it is good to understand more about the background of aggression in dogs.
In general there are two different types of aggressive behaviour:
The anxious-aggressive dog and the dominant-aggressive dog. An anxious-aggressive dog can be recognised by its pulled back ears and its low position. It will have pulled in its lips, showing its teeth. This dog is aggressive because it is very frightened and feels cornered. It would prefer to run away, but if it cannot then it will bite to defend itself. It will grab its victim anywhere it can. The attack is usually brief and as soon as the dog can see a way to escape, it is gone. In a confrontation with other dogs, it will normally turn out to be the loser. It can become even more aggressive once it has realised that people or other dogs are afraid of it. This behaviour cannot be corrected just like that. First you have to try and understand what the dog is afraid of. Professional advice is a good idea here. The wrong approach can easily make the problem worse.

The dominant-aggressive dog's body language is different. Its ears stand up and its tail is raised and stiff. This dog will always go for its victim's arms, legs or throat. It is extremely self-assured and highly placed in the dog hierarchy. Its attack is a display of power rather than a consequence of fear. This dog needs to know who is the boss. You must bring it up rigorously and with a strong hand. An obedience course can help.

A dog may also bite when it is in pain. This is a natural defensive reaction. In this case try to resolve the dog's fear as far as possible. Reward it for letting you get to the painful spot. Be careful, because a dog in pain may also bite its master! Muzzling it can help to prevent problems in case you have to do something that may be painful. Never punish a dog for this type of aggression!

Fear

The source of anxious behaviour can often be traced to the first weeks of a dog's life. A shortage of new experiences during the important socialisation phase has great influence on its later behaviour. A dog that never encountered humans, other dogs or animals during this period will be afraid of them later. This fear is common in dogs brought up in a barn or kennel, with almost no contact with humans. As we saw, fear can lead to aggressive behaviour, so it is important that a puppy gets as many new impressions as possible in the first weeks of its life. Take it with you into town in the car or on the bus, walk with it down busy streets and allow it to have plenty of contact with humans, other dogs and other animals.

It is a huge task to turn an anxious, poorly socialised dog into a real pet. It will probably take an enourmous amount of attention, love, patience and energy to get this animal

used to everything around it. Reward it often and give it plenty of time to adapt and, over time, it will learn to trust you and become less anxious. Try not to force anything, because this will always have the reverse effect. Here too, an obedience class can help a lot. A dog can be especially afraid of strangers. Have visitors give it something tasty as a treat. Put a can of dog biscuits by the door so that your visitors can spoil your dog when they arrive. Here again, do not try to force anything. If the dog is still frightened, leave it in peace.

Dogs are often frightened in certain situations; well-known examples are thunderstorms and fireworks. In these cases try to ignore their anxious behaviour.
If you react to a dog's whimpering and whining, it is the same as rewarding it. If you ignore its fear completely, the dog will quickly learn that nothing is wrong. You can speed up this 'learning process' by rewarding its positive behaviour.

Rewarding

Rewarding forms the basis for bringing up a dog. Rewarding good behaviour works far better than punishing bad behaviour and rewarding is also more fun than punishment. Over time the opinions on how to bring up dogs have gradually changed. In the past the proper way to correct bad behaviour was a sharp pull on the lead. Today, experts view rewarding as a positive incentive to get dogs to do what we expect of them. There are many ways to reward a dog. The usual ways are a pat or a friendly word, even without a tasty treat to go with it. Of course, a piece of dog biscuit does wonders when you are training a puppy. Be sure you always have something delicious in your pocket to reward good behaviour. Another form of reward is play. Whenever a dog notices that you have a ball in your pocket, it will not go far from your side. As soon as you have finished playing, put the ball away. In this way your dog will always do its best in exchange for a game.

Despite the emphasis you put on rewarding good behaviour, a dog can sometimes be a nuisance or disobedient. You must correct such behaviour immediately. Always be consistent; once 'no' must always mean 'no'.

Barking

Dogs which bark too much and too often are a nuisance for their surroundings. A dog owner may tolerate barking up to a point, but neighbours are often annoyed by the unnecessary noise. Shih Tzu are not particularly noisy, so do not encourage your puppy to bark and yelp. Of course, it should be able to announce its presence, but if it goes on barking it must be called to order with a strict 'Quiet!'. If a puppy fails to obey, just hold its muzzle closed with your hand.

A dog will sometimes bark for long periods when left alone. It feels threatened and tries to get someone's attention by barking. There are special training programmes for this problem, where dogs learn that being alone is nothing to be afraid of, and that their master will always return.

You can practise this with your dog at home. Leave the room and come back in at once. Reward your dog if it stays quiet. Gradually increase the length of your absences and keep rewarding it as long as it remains quiet. Never punish the dog if it does bark or yelp. It will never understand punishment afterwards, and this will only make the problem worse. Never go back into the room as long as your dog is barking, as it will view this as a reward. You might want to make the dog feel more comfortable by switching the radio on for company during your absence. It will eventually learn that you always come back and the barking will reduce. If you do not get the required result, attend an obedience course or consult a behaviour therapist.

Breeding

Dogs, and thus Shih Tzu, follow their instincts, and reproduction is one of nature's important processes. For people who enjoy breeding dogs this is a positive circumstance.

Those who simply want a cosy companion, however, do not need the regular adventures with females on heat and unrestrainable males.
Knowing a little about breeding dogs will help you to understand why they behave the way they do, and the measures you need to take when this happens.

Liability

Breeding dogs is more than simply 1+1= many. If you are planning to breed with your Shih Tzu, be on your guard, otherwise the whole affair can turn into a financial drama because, under the law, a breeder is liable for the quality of his puppies.

The breed clubs place strict conditions on animals used for breeding. They must be examined for possible congenital defects (see chapter *Health*). This is the breeder's first obligation, and if you breed a litter and sell the puppies without these checks having been made, you can be held liable by the new owners for any costs arising from any inherited defects. These veterinary costs can be enormous! So contact the breed association in case you plan to breed a litter of Shih Tzu.

The female in season

Bitches become sexually mature at about eight to twelve months. Then they go into season for the first time. They are on heat for two to three weeks. During the first ten days they discharge little drops of blood and they become steadily more attractive to males. The bitch is fertile during the second half of her season, and will accept a male to mate. The best time for mating is then between the tenth and thirteenth day of her season. A female's first season is often shorter and less severe than those that follow. If you do want to breed with your female you must allow this first and sometimes the second season to pass. Most bitches go into season twice per year.

If you do plan to breed with your Shih Tzu in the future, then spaying is not an option to prevent unwanted offspring. A temporary solution is a contraceptive injection, although this is controversial because of possible side effects such as womb infections and the possibility of mamilla tumours when the female gets older.

Phantom pregnancy

A phantom pregnancy is a not uncommon occurrence. The female behaves as if she has a litter. She takes all kinds of things to her basket and treats them like puppies. Her teats swell up and sometimes milk is actually produced. The female will sometimes behave aggressively towards humans or other animals, as if she is defending her young. Phantom pregnancies usually begin two months after a season and can last a number of weeks.
If it happens to a bitch once, it will often then occur after every season.
If this is a problem, spaying is the best solution, because continual phantom pregnancies increase the risk of womb or teat conditions. In the short term a hormone treatment is worth trying, also perhaps giving the animal homeopathic medicines.
Camphor can give relief when teats are heavily swollen, but rubbing the teats with ice or a cold cloth (moisten and freeze) can also help relieve the pain. Feed the female less than usual, and make sure she gets enough attention and extra exercise.

Preparing to breed

If you do plan to breed a litter of puppies, you must first wait for your female to be physically and mentally full-grown. In any event you must let her first season pass. As early as possible, some time before the bitch is expected to go into season, start the search for a potential mate. If your female is registered, and has passed all the health checks (see the chapter *Health*). The breeding club will help to find a suitable dog. If you plan to mate your bitch with a dog not on The Kennel Club list, think about the following.

- Do not pick a dog without a pedigree.
- Let the owner confirm that he does not display any congenital defects.
- Observe the dog's character and temperament and look for characteristics that will reinforce the positive qualities of your bitch and compensate for any of her weak points or defective personality traits.
- Never breed two extremes together. If both parents are hyperactive, for example, there is a high chance that this (undesirable) trait will be even stronger in their offspring.

The owner of the dog will expect a certain amount as a cover fee. Sometimes a pup from the future litter may be the fee. Before mating your bitch, check that she is free of any parasites (external and internal). She must be fit, not overweight and vaccinated against all the usual diseases. If you want strong, healthy puppies, the mother-to-be must be in optimal condition. As soon as the female shows the first signs of being on heat, make an appointment with the owner of the male for the first mating attempt. In most cases, after

the first apparently successful attempt at mating, the bitch is brought to the dog again after two or three days.

Pregnancy

It is often difficult to tell at first when a bitch is pregnant. Only after about four weeks you can feel the pups in her womb. She will now slowly get fatter and her behaviour will usually change. Her teats will swell up during the last few weeks of pregnancy. The average pregnancy lasts 63 days, and costs the bitch more and more in terms of energy. In the beginning she should be fed her normal amount of food, but her nutritional needs increase in jumps during the second half of the pregnancy. Give her approximately fifteen percent more food each week from the fifth week on. The mother-to-be needs extra energy and proteins during this phase of her pregnancy. (See chapter on *Feeding*)

During the last weeks you can give her a concentrated food, rich in energy, such as dry puppy food. Divide this into several small portions per day, because she can no longer deal with large portions of food. Towards the end of the pregnancy, her energy needs can easily be one-and-a-half times more than usual.
After about seven weeks the mother will demonstrate nesting behaviour and begin to look for a place to give birth to her pups. This might be her own basket or a special birthing box. This must be ready at least one week before the birth to give the mother time to get used to it. The basket or box should preferably be in a quiet place.

Birth

A litter of Shih Tzu consists of four to five puppies. The birth usually passes without problems. Of course, you should be in the area during the whole process and the mother

will feel more relaxed due to your presence. Intervention is rarely needed but, of course, contact your vet immediately if you suspect a problem!

Suckling

After the birth, the mother starts to produce milk. The suckling period is very demanding. During the first three to four weeks the pups rely entirely on their mother's milk. During this time she needs extra food and fluids. This can be up to three or four times the normal amount. If she's producing too little milk, you can give both the mother and her pups special puppy milk. Here too, divide the high quantity of food the mother needs over several smaller portions. Again, choose a concentrated, high-energy, food and give her plenty of fresh drinking water, but not cow's milk, which can cause diarrhoea. You can start to give the pups some extra food from the third week. Start with specially designed starter food that matches very well with their mother's milk and can easily be eaten with the milk teeth from puppies. You start with one meal of starter food per week, which you gradually increase by one meal per week.
When the puppies are seven weeks old, they should be fully weaned, i.e. they no longer drink their mother's milk. The mother's milk production gradually stops and her food needs also drop. Within a couple of weeks after weaning, the mother should again be getting the same amount of food as before the pregnancy.

When you feed your puppies, make sure that each pup gets its fair share. If you feel that one pup is missing out, set it apart when feeding but do this only as long as necessary and get it eating with its brothers and sisters as quickly as possible.

Only that way will it learn to fend for itself. Over-eating is just as dangerous as under-eating, so increase the amount gradually. Watch for the growth and behaviour of the pups and regularly check that their stools are properly formed. Small hard stools can be a sign of malnutrition or lack of fluids. Stools that are too soft or runny are often caused by overfeeding.

Neutering and spaying

As soon as you are sure your bitch should never bear a (new) litter spaying is the best solution. During spaying, the uterus is surgically removed. The bitch no longer goes into season and can never become pregnant. The best age for a spaying is about eighteen months, when the bitch is more or less fully grown.

A male dog may also be neutered for medical reasons or to correct undesirable sexual behaviour. During neutering the testicles are removed, which is a simple procedure and usually without complications. There is no special age for neutering. Where possible, wait until the dog is fully grown.

Vasectomy is sufficient where it is only a case of making the dog infertile. In this case the dog keeps its sexual drive but can no longer reproduce.

Sports and shows

A Shih Tzu is an energetic dog and likes to be busy. It likes to do something together with its boss.
Many kennel clubs run their own championships. If you regularly participate in activities with your Shih Tzu, you will not only realise that the bond between master and dog has grown stronger, but also that your dog is quieter and more obedient at home.

Behaviour and obedience

You can pick from a whole range of obedience training courses, beginning with a puppy course. Shih Tzu usually enjoy this type of course. After elementary obedience courses, you can train your dog for various behaviour and obedience diplomas.

Obedience

You can follow up on basic obedience training by trying to pass the Behaviour and Obedience diplomas, classes 1, 2 & 3, with increasing degrees of difficulty. This discipline is also practised in a competitive environment, and there are British, European and World Championships. Among other things, the dog must walk on the lead, follow at foot off the lead, stay standing or sit or lie for a set time while its master walks away and is out of sight for several minutes. Tracking and retrieving is trained and tested almost to perfection.

The British form of Obedience goes a step further; the accent here is on perfect performance of the set tasks. Highly intensive training is intended to make dog and master one unit, which, during the execution of several exercises, seems to be glued together. Obedience is only performed in competition, there are no diplomas.

Road safety

Especially useful are road safety courses for dogs. Here, your Shih Tzu can learn a few obedience exercises and at the end of the course can show you how safely it conducts itself in traffic.

Shows

Visiting a show is highly recommended if you want to learn more about a certain breed. You will also be able to get into direct contact with breeders and other owners. Showing animals is a very competitive sport, in which breeders and exhibitors invest a lot of time. Some breeders even dedicate their life to this. There are many things to be considered. You need to choose which shows to enter and what you need to achieve for the dog to be awarded a title. The entry forms, payments, hotel reservations, everything needs to be taken care of well in advance. If you want to make a good appearance in the ring with your dog, you should also find appropriate clothing for yourself.

Of course, most important of all is your dog itself. Showing a dog requires a lot of preparation. You cannot simply start preparing your dog a few weeks before the show, but you must start to prepare it for a show career when it is still very young, as it takes a lot of training until a dog presents itself well.

For some breeds, many dogs compete in the classes, and this will make it a lot more difficult to win a title. Sometimes, the representative of a very rare breed may be crowned Champion, without the dog ever having competed against another one of its kind. It is also possible for the judge to withhold the award. In order to become Champion your dog needs to have three Challenge Certificates awarded by three different judges. Of those three, at least one should be achieved when the dog is twelve months or older. Challenge Certificates can also be awarded to the best of each sex in a breed. The British system allows a certain number of dogs per breed to be awarded the Challenge Certificate. The annual limit of Challenge Certificates to be awarded to representatives of a certain breed may be 30 or just 6.

When the dogs enter the ring, the judge looks at them very carefully. Each dog is examined visually and by hand. The breed standards of many dog breeds contain

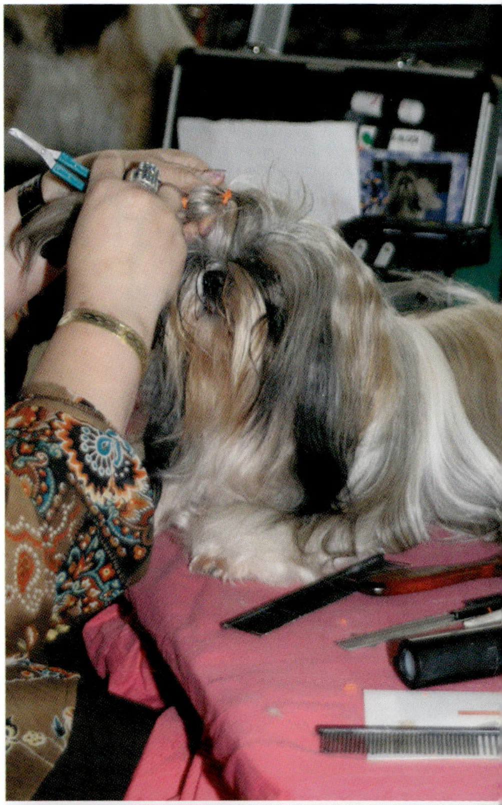

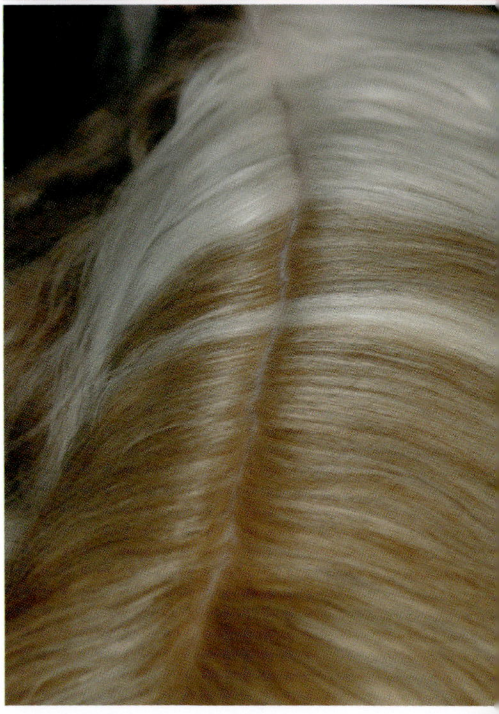

remarks regarding the build. The teeth will also be examined, as each breed standard will have its own notes regarding an undershot jaw or scissor bite. It is understandable that the judge will need to feel the dog in order to fully compare it to the breed standard. The breed standards also contain notes on gait and movement, which is why the judge will also need to see your dog move. Judges also pay attention to the way a dog carries its head and tail.

Ring craft classes

Here you are taught how to prepare yourself and your dog in the best possible way to take part in a show and how to present your dog when the big day has finally arrived. After these ring craft classes you should be able to show your dog in a way that it makes the best possible impression in the ring and with the judge. It is a good idea to first visit a show as a spectator, so that you get to know the procedure of a show.
There are usually several classes, e.g. one for puppies and one for more experienced dogs. The classes are usually very sociable events, where training is combined with lots of fun. It is not easy to teach a dog and its master all the tricks of showing. Even if you do not plan to follow a showing career with your dog, it is still a good idea to take it to a course. Your dog will learn to socialize with people that it does not know and with other dogs. It will also learn to walk on the lead properly without being distracted.
Some clubs which organise ring craft classes also organise friendly unofficial shows and Companion Dog Shows for their members once in a while.

Dog Clubs

There is a large number of dog clubs in the UK. For more information, look on the site of The Kennel Club, and click on the Breed Standard button.

Types of Shows

There are different types of shows, of which we will give a very brief overview here. Single Breed Shows (for one breed only, organised by a breed club)

- Companion Dog Shows (for charitable causes)
- Open Shows (you can qualify for Crufts at some of these shows)
- Championship Shows (the most prestigious shows, often the possibility to qualify for Crufts and to attain Challenge Certificates).

Of course, your dog must look very smart for the show. The judge will not be impressed if its coat is not clean and its paws are dirty. Nails must be clipped and the teeth must be free of plaque.

The dog must also be free from parasites and ailments. Apart from those things, judges also hate badly brought up dogs, anxious or nervous dogs. Get into touch with the local dog club or the breed association if you want to know more about dog shows.

Do not forget!

If you are planning to take your dog to a club match or in fact to any show, you need to be well prepared. Do not forget the following:

For yourself:

- Show documents if they have been sent to you
- Food and drink
- Clip for the catalogue number
- Chairs if an outdoor show

For your dog:

- Food and water bowls and food
- Rewarding treats
- Dog blanket and perhaps a cushion
- Show lead
- Grooming equipment
- A benching chain and collar

Parasites

All dogs are vulnerable to various sorts of parasites. Parasites are tiny creatures that live at the expense of another animal. They feed on blood, skin and other body substances.
There are two main types. Internal parasites live within their host animal's body (tapeworm and roundworm for example) and external parasites live on the animal's exterior, usually in its coat (fleas, lice and ticks), but also in its ears (ear mite).

Fleas

Fleas feed on a dog's blood. They cause not only itching and skin problems, but can also carry infections such as tapeworm. In large numbers they can cause anaemia and dogs can also become allergic to a flea's saliva, which can cause serious skin conditions. So it is important to treat your dog against fleas as effectively as possible, do not just treat the dog itself but also its surroundings. For treatment of the animal, there are various medicines: drops for the neck, drops to put in its food, flea collars, long-life sprays and flea powders. There are various sprays in pet shops that can be used to eradicate fleas in the dog's immediate surroundings. Choose a spray that kills both adult fleas and their larvae. If your dog goes into your car, you should spray that too. Fleas can also affect other pets, so you should treat those too. When spraying a room, cover any aquariums or fishbowls. If the spray reaches the water, it can be fatal for your fish! Switch off the oxygen pump for one hour. During and directly after spraying the room no pets are allowed there. To protect yourself you should cover your mouth and nose. Your veterinarian and pet shop have a wide range of flea-treatments and can advise you on this subject.

Ticks

Ticks are small, spider-like parasites. They feed on the blood of the animal or person they have settled on. A tick looks like a tiny, grey-coloured leather bag with eight feet. When it has sucked itself full, it can easily be five to ten times its own size and be darker in colour. Dogs usually fall victim to ticks in bushes, woods or long grass. Ticks cause not only irritation by their blood-sucking, but can also carry a number of serious diseases. This applies especially to the Mediterranean countries, where ticks can be infected with blood parasites. In our country these diseases are fortunately less common. Unfortunately Lyme disease, which can also affect human beings, has reached our shores as well. Your veterinarian can prescribe a special treatment if you are planning to take your dog to southern Europe. It is important to fight ticks as effectively as possible. Check your dog regularly, especially when it has been running free in woods and bushes. Your dog can also wear an anti-tick collar.

Flea

Tick

Removing a tick is simple when using tick tweezers. Grip the tick with the tweezers, very close to the dog's skin and carefully pull it out. You can also grip the tick between your fingers and by using a turning movement, pull it carefully out. You must disinfect the spot where the tick had been, by using iodine to prevent infection. Never soak the tick in alcohol, ether or oil. In a shock reaction the tick may discharge the infected contents of its stomach into the dog's skin and infect your dog.

Ear-mites

Itchy ears are sometimes a symptom of ear-mites. Ear-mites are small parasites that cause a severe irritation in the ear and are easily passed from dog to dog (and to cat). The vet must start the treatment by carefully cleaning away the wax from inside the ear. You will have to follow up on this with the application of prescribed medication. All animals in the household must be treated at the same time.

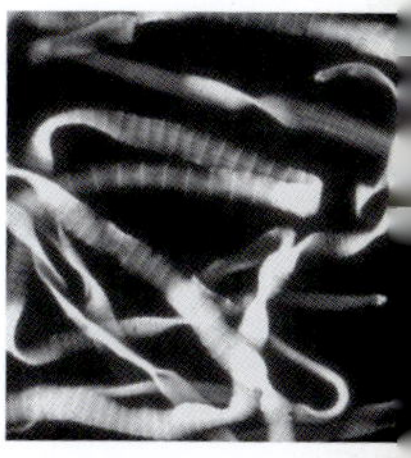

Tapeworm

Roundworm

Worms

Dogs can suffer from various types of worm. The most common ones are tapeworm and roundworm. Tapeworm causes diarrhoea and poor general condition. With a tapeworm infection you can sometimes find small pieces of the worm around the dog's anus or on its bed. In this case, the dog must be wormed. You should also check your dog for fleas, which carry the tapeworm infection. Roundworm is a condition that reoccurs regularly. Puppies always are infected through their mother's milk. Your vet has medicines to prevent roundworm. Roundworm causes problems such as diarrhoea, loss of weight and stagnated growth, particularly in younger dogs. You might find roundworms in the faeces of the dog. In serious cases the pup becomes thin, but with a swollen belly. It may vomit and you can then see the worms in its vomit. They are spaghetti-like tendrils. A puppy must be treated against worms every two weeks from its 3rd week onwards until it is three months old. When the puppy has reached the age of three months, it has to be treated every three months during its first year. Adult dogs should be treated every six months. And of course when you notice that your dog is infected by worms, you treat it more often.

Health

We now go into some medical ups and downs of the Shih Tzu. We want to give some brief information about ailments and disorders that affect this breed more than other dogs.

Breed-specific conditions

Fortunately, most Shih Tzus are healthy and happy dogs that can live to the age of fifteen years. We want to inform you about some breed-specific conditions of the Shih Tzu that are listed here below.

Eyes

The relatively large, frontally set eyes of the Shih Tzu are prone to infections and injuries. It is not recommended to walk a Shih Tzu in the forests or in the high grass. After each walk, the eyes should be checked carefully for the presence of seeds or stalks. Additionally, the eyes must be rinsed daily with normal saline (physiological salt solution). In case of any irritation and/or excessive discharge, you should immediately ask a veterinarian for advice.

Cataracts

This condition causes a clouding of the cornea. It can be noticed when a dog's eye is of any other colour than green when you look at it in artificial light. Cataract can be hereditary and appear in young animals, sometimes as early as at an age of eight weeks; it is passed on by both parents. More frequently it is a result of injury or diseases. An ophthalmoscopic examination by a qualified eye-vet can determinate the type of cataract. Dogs with hereditary cataract should not be used for breeding purposes.

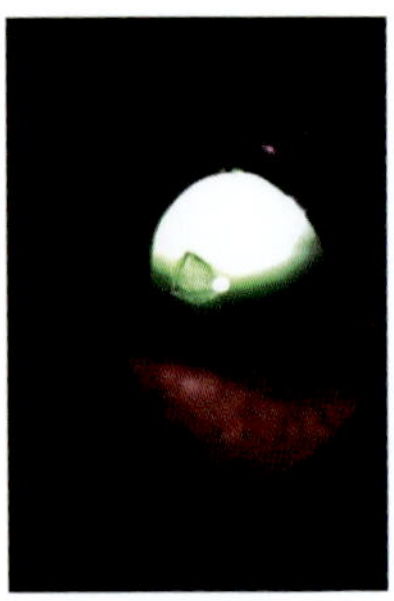

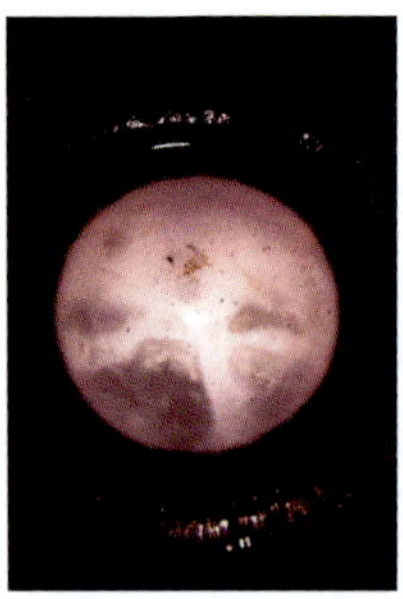

Left:
early stage cataract

Right:
advanced stage cataract

Cleft palate

Though rarely, it may happen that a puppy is born with a smaller or larger opening in its palate. Such puppies show difficulties in sucking and – when doing so – one can notice small bubbles of milk coming out of the nostrils. In the most severe cases, the affected puppies fade away and die within a few days. The condition seems to be hereditary, but the mode of inheritance remains unknown. Checking the mouths of newborn puppies should be a part of the routine examination by the veterianarian.

Tight nostrils

This appears to be an inherited condition. The most severe cases can be noticed at birth, when the nostrils are so tight that the nose is deformed. Affected puppies usually die within a few days. Less severe cases do not become evident until the third week and an affected puppy shows obvious difficulties in breathing. It will die unless fed by hand and kept in a constant, high temperature. Usually this condition lasts for about two weeks and gradually improves to normal.

Familial nephropathy

It is also known as kidney dysplasia and thought to be hereditary, although the mode of inheritance is still under research. Whole litters can be affected and the onset of the disease varies from several weeks up to one year. The main symptoms are excessive drinking and urinating. The disease is incurable and always fatal.

Schematic representation of the knee

Knee

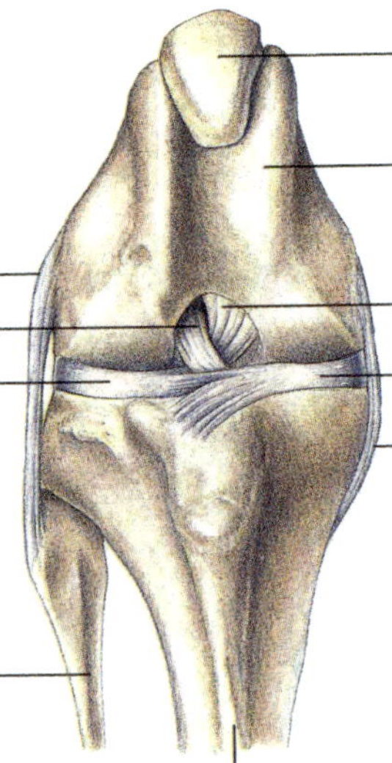

Patella luxation

In the case of this abnormality, the kneecap is not placed centrally at the end of the shinbone. The kneecap ends up next to the joint. A luxating kneecap can occur if the groove is not deep enough. This can be hereditary, but it can also be the result of trauma (an accident). In this case the luxation will be combined with ruptured ligaments. Patella luxation occurs in different severities. The amount of pain and discomfort varies per dog. If the luxation is of minor gradation it can be sufficient to move the attachment of the knee ligaments. If the groove of the femur is not deep enough it must be deepened. Nowadays techniques are chosen to save the cartilage. The joint can be made tighter in order to keep the kneecap better on its place.
Slippery floors and strange movements (such as running after balls too wildly, bouncing and quick turns) are not healthy for the joints of any dogs, whether they are big or small, puppies or adults.

Diseases caused by viruses and other organisms

Pseudo rabies

Pseudo rabies or Aujeszky's disease is actually a disease found in pigs. The virus is transferred to other animals when they eat raw pork which is infected. The disease affects the central nervous system. A dog which has been infected with the virus becomes restless, apathetic, nervous and loses its appetite. Aujeszky's disease progresses incredibly quickly: the animal will become paralysed and die within a week. There is no cure. Therefore never feed dogs (or other pets) raw or not properly cooked pork.

Corona

Corona is a viral disease, the symptoms of which are vomiting and diarrhoea. This disease looks like a parvo virus infection, but is less severe in its progress. Besides the

symptoms listed under parvo virus, other symptoms include damage to the mucous membranes, which manifests itself in eye and nose discharge. The disease is spread via faeces.

Hepatitis

Hepatitis is a highly infectious liver disease. The virus is found in both dogs and foxes. The noticeable symptoms vary widely. Approximately one week after infection, the body temperature increases, after which the animal's temperature starts to fluctuate.
The dog remains lively during the first few days, but this changes. Symptoms include: coughing and an inflamed throat, moist eyes, lack of appetite, sometimes in combination with vomiting and/or diarrhoea. The dog's eyes will cloud over. The virus is spread via the urine of infected dogs. As infected dogs urinate in parks and against trees, the disease spreads very quickly. Hepatitis symptoms vary from light fever to a very serious liver infection. If the disease is treated at an early stage, there is a chance of full recovery. If the liver is infected, the fever will run very high and the dog will no longer eat. Invariably, if the disease reaches this stage the dog will die. Hepatitis can cause young dogs and puppies to die very suddenly.
Hepatitis is not always easy to diagnose, as the symptoms are very similar to those of Carré's disease.

Carré's disease

This disease is caused by a virus and is highly infectious. The severity of the first symptoms, a runny nose and some coughing, is often underestimated. Shortly after that, fever, lack of appetite, vomiting and/or diarrhoea follow. Furthermore, the dog will suffer from an inflamed throat and pussy discharge from the nose and eyes, spasms and cramps. A young dog may suddenly become severely ill. The virus causes inflammation in the intestines, but also meningitis. Many dogs do not survive this disease. The dogs that do survive often suffer permanent nerve damage, or a 'tick'. Many dogs have behavioural disorders which they did not have before the infection, e.g. orientation problems. The disease is spread via saliva, urine and faeces.

Rabies

This viral disease is fatal to humans and dogs. The virus enters the body when saliva from an infected animal reaches a wound of a hitherto healthy animal. It spreads via nerves to the brain, and will eventually kill the animal. After being bitten by an infected animal, it can take up to 50 days before the new victim shows any symptoms. The final phase of this disease is terrible.

The brain is affected by the virus, the dog is terrified, hides in a corner, and its behaviour can suddenly switch, i.e. the sweetest dog may suddenly become feral and very aggressive. It will bite everything and attack anything that comes close to it. Luckily, rabies does not exist in the UK, but if you are planning to take your dog abroad, you should have it vaccinated against rabies. Rabies is spread via the saliva (bites) of foxes, badgers and other animals.

Kennel cough

The kennel cough syndrome is caused by a number of different micro-organisms: Para-influenza virus, Bordetella and others.

The disease usually spreads where many dogs are kept closely together, such as in a kennel, dog hotel, at a show or at dog schools. The symptoms of this respiratory problem are a harsh, rough cough and occasionally damage to the lungs.

Dogs do not usually become severely ill from kennel cough, but you must have your dog treated by a vet. Cough medicine (thyme syrup) can help to soften the mucous membranes and a holiday to a place with lots of fresh air can do wonders. If you are going to leave your dog in a boarding kennel, it is best (and usually also required) to have your dog vaccinated against kennel cough. You should have your dog vaccinated against this obnoxious cough approximately four weeks before it goes to kennels. The disease is spread via the breath.

Parvo virus

Parvo virus is a highly infectious viral disease. A dog infected with the parvo virus will usually not survive. The virus is spread via the faeces of an infected dog.

When a healthy dogs sniffs at these faeces, it becomes infected straight away. The virus penetrates to the intestines, where it causes serious inflammation. Within a very short time, the dog will suffer bloody diarrhoea, may vomit blood, become drowsy, develop a fever and become very seriously ill.

The dog will usually also not eat or drink and can therefore dehydrate. Treatment primarily consists of administering large amounts of fluid intravenously. Most dogs die within 48 hours after the first symptoms. In puppies, an infection with parvo virus can cause cardiac arrest. Nowadays, puppies are usually vaccinated against parvo virus very early in life. Puppies which have survived the disease may unfortunately die very suddenly later on due to angina.

Weil's disease

Weil's disease (leptospirosis) is a disease caused by micro-organisms. Dogs are most commonly infected in spring or autumn. In younger dogs, the disease can easily be fatal. Humans can also be infected through dogs or rats. A dog swimming in contaminated water might contract bacteria via the mucous membranes or tiny wounds on the skin. The bacteria gather in the liver and kidneys. The symptoms include: high fever, drowsiness and muscle pain. Furthermore, the dog suffers from a lack of appetite, vomiting and is very thirsty.

The dog may also suffer from nose bleeds, dark urine and sometimes yellow fever. The disease is spread via the urine of infected rats and dogs.

First aid for dogs

When your dog gets injured or ill, the time that passes before professional medical help is available can be crucial. Whatever you do or do not do in this time can save your pet's life.
Bear in mind that the first aid you apply is only intended to gain control over acute emergency situations. Your dog may have suffered internal injuries, which you cannot see. Therefore always take your dog to a veterinarian for examination!

If you are in any doubt about anything, ask your vet for advice. He will certainly understand if you are uncertain about what to do. Applying medical aid to an animal always has one complication: communication with the patient. You cannot explain to a dog that you are trying to help it and lessen its pain. A seriously injured animal is scared and in a lot of pain. It will therefore often try to escape or to attack its helper(s). You must therefore restrain the dog so that you do not get hurt. At the same time, you must make it clear to the animal, through a firm but friendly approach, that you are in control of the situation, but still sympathetic. Keep on talking calmly and frequently address the animal by its name. The tone of your voice and hearing its name will have a calming, relaxing effect. Lay or sit the dog on a table. This makes it more difficult for the animal to escape and it makes treatment easier for you.
Not all cases requiring first aid are the same. One situation may be more severe than another and may require quicker intervention. There is a fixed order of treatment, from very severe to less severe. It is therefore very important to stick to this order when

treating wounds and conditions: a beautiful support bandage will not do any good if the victim died in the meantime because it could not breathe anymore. In the overview below you will see which life functions must be restored first, before you begin with treating the next function.

Order of treatment
1. Respiration
2. Heart function
3. Blood vessels
4. Shock
5. Poisoning
6. Fractures
7 Digestive tract
8. Other injuries

1. Respiration

Together with the heart function, breathing is an animal's most important vital function. By breathing, oxygen is absorbed into the body, which is necessary to allow the organs and tissues to function properly. If an oxygen deficit goes on for too long, the organs and tissues will become damaged very quickly and eventually die off. If respiration stops, the animal is in acute danger. A dog with breathing difficulties often stretches its neck and tries to inhale air with all its might. The mucous membranes of the tongue and the eyes turn blue and the animal will become unconscious after a while. If your dog is lying absolutely still and you cannot see anything on first sight, check the breathing by laying your hand or a few fingers on the chest: you should feel it moving up and down.

If your dog is suffering from breathing difficulties, take it to fresh air immediately. Try to get behind the cause of the breathing difficulties as quickly as possible and eliminate it as soon as you can. Remove any possibly obstructing objects from the neck (collars, flea collars). Check that no objects are stuck in the throat or windpipe. Do not be too careful, as every second counts now! In some cases you can apply a short thrust on the chest and push the object out with the air from the lungs. Applying pressure on the outside of the throat will also sometimes help.

If the dog is choking on water, you need to lift it up by its back legs with the head hanging down. This allows the fluid to drain from the lungs. Then push on the chest a few times to remove the last remaining fluid from the lungs.

If the breathing still does not pick up, you will need to apply mouth-to-mouth resuscitation to your dog. Try to take the victim to the veterinarian as quickly as possible. Continuing to apply mouth-to-mouth resuscitation during the journey.

Possible causes of respiratory problems:

- Too little oxygen in the environment (insufficient ventilation, plastic bag, box);
- Water, gas or smoke in the lungs (drowning, carbon monoxide, fire);
- Swallowed objects, swelling of the mucous membranes in the respiratory tract (asthmatic attack, inflammation), swelling of the tongue (wasp's sting);
- Restricted throat (collar, flea collar);
- Damage to the diaphragm, broken ribs;
- Damaged lungs;
- Suffocating on food (through fright) or vomit.

Loss of consciousness

A dog can lose its consciousness for a number of reasons. Epilepsy, a heavy blow, brain haemorrhaging and poisoning are some possibilities. Loss of consciousness is always an emergency, in which case you need to act as follows:

- Get someone to notify the vet straight away;
- Lay the dog on its side, as long as you cannot detect a wound there, with the paws pointing away from the body. The head needs to lay somewhat higher than the rest of the body;
- Check the pulse. If necessary, apply heart massage.
- Check the respiration. If necessary, apply mouth-to-mouth resuscitation;
- When the dog is breathing (again), pull its tongue out of its mouth and remove any food remains;
- Do not give the victim food or water;
- Keep the animal warm with a blanket.

2. Heart function

A dog can also suffer a heart attack. Not every heart attack results in cardiac arrest. Some causes of heart attacks include drowning, suffocation, poisoning, severe allergic reaction, trauma or electric shock.

Symptoms include pain, shortness of breath, nausea or vomiting and dizziness.

Do not think that it will pass over. If you suspect heart failure, you must take your dog to the veterinarian as quickly as possible.

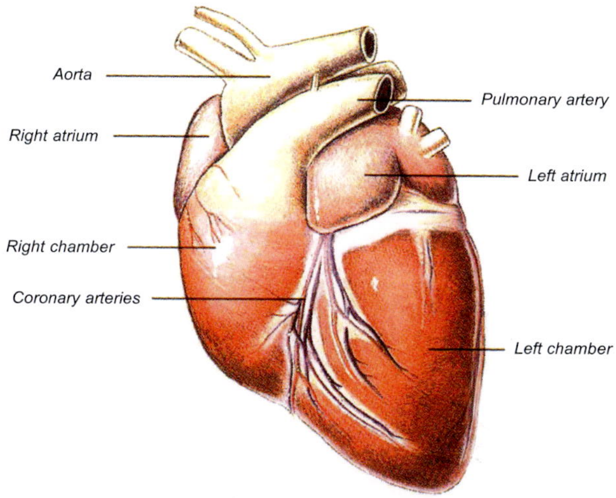

Above: schematic representation of the heart

Below: cross-sectional view of the heart

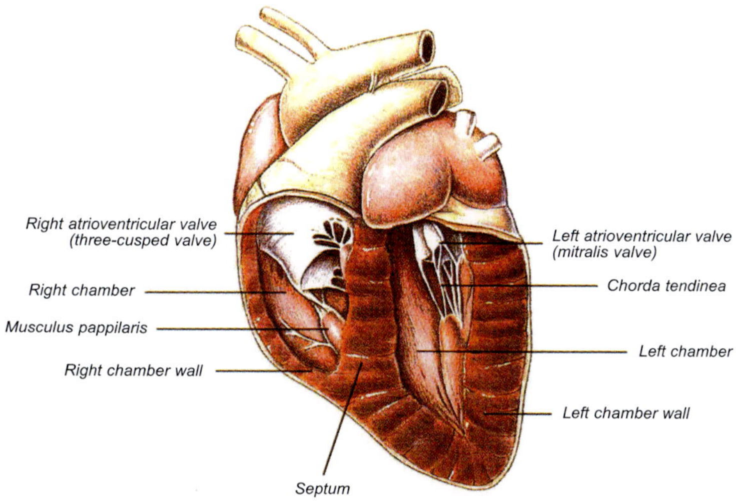

3. Blood vessels

Bleeding

A dog can become injured and lose blood. In the case of serious blood loss, the animal may die. How much blood is lost and how quickly depends on the size of the wound, but also on the type of blood vessel. We differentiate between three types of bleeding, depending on the type of blood vessel injured:

Capillary bleeding

This is a fairly harmless bleeding; however, it does need to be treated. The wound is not deep (often only a scrape) and there is little loss of blood. Disinfect the wound well. Briefly press it closed with some gauze. You often do not even need to dress it.

Venous bleeding

In this type of bleeding the blood streams out of the wound steadily and is dark red in colour. This is because the blood is flowing towards the heart through the veins and is low in oxygen. Clean the wound well with a disinfectant tissue or sterile gauze soaked in boiled water and then dress it. Take your dog to the veterinarian straight away. He will again disinfect the wound thoroughly and stitch it if necessary.

Arterial bleeding

This is a very serious type of bleeding, which can be fatal for your dog. The blood gushes out of the wound intermittently and is light red in colour. This is because it comes straight from the heart and contains a lot of oxygen. The victim loses a lot of blood in a very short time. You therefore need to act very quickly:

- Hold the dog with a restraining grip and try to calm it. Use your voice to prevent it losing consciousness.
- First check respiration and pulse, and try to stop the bleeding after that.
- Lay the bleeding part of the body higher than the rest of the body.
- Put some sterile gauze or a clean cloth on the wound, and exert pressure with the palm of your hand, so that the blood vessel is squeezed tight. If necessary, put some

extra gauze or cotton wool on the wound and exert more pressure. On spots where the skin is loose (lips, cheeks, scruff), tightly push the wound edges together in your fist.
- When the bleeding has stopped, put a thick layer of cotton wool on the gauze or cloth. Bandage the wound with a tight bandage. Keep on exerting pressure.
- Take the animal to the veterinarian as quickly as possible.

Major bleeding at the foot or tail can be stopped by exerting pressure on one of the so-called pressure points with your finger. These are points where the blood vessels run closely under the skin and are easily squeezed tight.

If you cannot manage to stop arterial bleeding in the manner described above, you can apply a tourniquet as a last resort. A tourniquet must never be applied around the neck or head! After applying a tourniquet, take the victim to the veterinarian as quickly as possible. Be aware that a dog can go into shock as a result of serious bleeding.

Minor cut and stab wounds:
- Hold the victim in a restraining grip. It will probably try to resist.
- Wash your hands thoroughly and use sterile material from a first aid kit as much as possible.
- Remove any hairs that might be in the wound: dampen them with clean water, stroke them out of the wound and cut them off close to the skin. Examine the depth of the wound.
- Rinse the wound clean with a mild disinfectant, which is dissolved in water. You can also dissolve two teaspoons of salt in a litre of tap water. Try to gently rub open small deep stab wounds.
- Wash the skin around the wound with disinfectant shampoo. Cover the wound with sterile gauze, to prevent suds getting in. Rinse with plenty of clean water afterwards.
- With graze wounds, in particular, there may be (a lot of) dirt in the skin. Remove it with a cotton bud or a corner of a clean cloth. Be very careful when doing this!
- Dab the wound dry with a clean, non-fluffy cloth.
- Put disinfectant salve on the wound and bandage it.
- Change the dressing every day and pay close attention to possible wound infections.
- If a scab has formed, you need to prevent the animal removing it. Keep the wound edges supple with Vaseline or cod-liver oil salve.

Major cuts or skin parts missing:
- In these cases your first aid attempts must be directed towards getting the animal to the veterinarian as quickly as possible, and to preventing the situation from worsening.

- The dog might be in a lot of pain. If necessary, apply a restraining grip.
- Remove any big objects, such as splinters, stones and twigs, from the wound. Do not remove objects that have penetrated deeply into the skin. If they stick far out of the wound, cut them off above the skin.
- Soak a clean cloth in a solution of two teaspoons of salt in one litre of water. Lay the wet cloth on the wound and fixate it with tape or bandage clamps.
- Keep the cloth wet with the saline solution during the transport to the veterinarian.
- Make sure that the animal cannot lick or bite at the wound.
- A big cut needs to be stitched by a vet within six hours. This will speed up the healing process.

A dog can also encounter wounds when the skin is still intact. Examples of this are bruises or haemorrhages. You can treat these by applying ice cubes which are wrapped in a tea towel. Your dog can also suffer more serious, internal damage. Symptoms include lightening of the mucous membranes and/or bloody discharge of slime from the nose. In the case of internal injuries, you must not move your dog or let it drink: call a vet straight away!

Burns

The skin is a very important organ for any animal. It protects the body against damaging external influences by giving it the right signals (e.g. it is warm, something is pinching). The skin also sends signals from the animal to its surroundings, e.g. hairs standing up. The coat is covered with aromatic substances, sweat and fats which come from the skin. Finally the skin also regulates the body's temperature and the dog's water balance: it makes sure that the body does not dehydrate in a warm environment. Burns can have serious consequences, especially when major parts of the skin have been affected. In these cases the skin can no longer fulfil its vital functions.

In the case of burns you always need to apply first aid. The animal will be in a lot of pain and will need to be examined by a vet as soon as possible. He will judge if the animal can be saved. Whether an animal can recover depends on the percentage of skin damaged and on how deeply the damage penetrates the skin.

In the case of burns you can try to prevent the condition worsening by thoroughly cooling off the animal as quickly as possible. Proceed as follows:

- Cool the burnt part of the skin with cold water as soon as possible (if necessary by dumping the victim in a pond or bucket). The cold not only alleviates the pain, but also gets the warmth out of the skin, which prevents deeper skin layers being seriously damaged.
- You need to cool off the dog for at least ten minutes. Carefully dab dry the area around the affected spot, but do not touch the wound: the risk of infection is too great.
- Do not put any salve or grease on the wound.
- Cover the wound with a clean cloth soaked in a solution of two teaspoons of salt in a litre of water. Keep the cloth damp with this solution during your drive to the veterinarian.
- Give the dog small amounts of water - if it can still swallow - over small time intervals (the mucous membranes of the throat and mouth may have been affected by the smoke).

- Burnt skin can no longer contain body warmth, which means that the dog may shake because of the cold. Keep it warm with a blanket.
- Even if your dog is obviously in a lot of pain: never feed it painkillers or sedatives of your own accord.

Bite wounds
It can happen that your dog gets bitten by a feral animal, such as a fox or a stray cat or dog. First of all, you should clean the wound with disinfectant. Take your dog to the veterinarian as quickly as possible for further treatment!

4. Shock

Shock is not actually a condition as such, but can be the result of serious injuries combined with severe blood loss, a bad fright and pain. An injured animal may also become stressed by your attempts to treat it, which can also easily lead to shock. Preventing shock is actually more important than treating it. In the case of shock, too little blood is pumped through the body. If this carries on for long, tissues and organs do not receive enough oxygen. This means that they can die off. If the brain gets insufficient oxygen, the animal will lose consciousness.
In cases where there is a real chance of the dog going into shock, you need to act as follows: Free the respiratory tract by pulling the tongue a little out of the mouth. Check first if there are any objects in the throat or mouth. If necessary, apply mouth-to-mouth resuscitation and/or heart massage and stop any bleeding. An animal with very high fever or heatstroke (sunstroke) needs to be cooled with cold, wet cloths applied to the head and neck. Bring the animal into quiet, dark surroundings. Make sure that the head is positioned a little higher than the rest of the body. In case of shock keep the animal

warm with a blanket and maybe with a hot water bottle (maximum 45°C). Alternatively, in the case of sunstroke keep it cool.
If the animal can still drink, give it small amounts of water. Never offer it anything to drink if there is any suspicion of internal damage! Take the animal to the veterinarian as quickly as possible. He will put it on a drip to stabilise the blood pressure.

Causes of shock:
- Cardiac arrest
- Severe bleeding
- Dehydration
- Bad fright
- Severe pain
- Poisoning
- Allergies
- Brain trauma
- Serious burns
- Severe stress
- Malignant tumours
- Septicaemia
- Sunstroke
- High fever
- Prolonged vomiting/ diarrhoea

Speedy actions can prevent the animal actually going into shock! If you see the following symptoms, you need to apply first aid immediately:
- Weak, irregular pulse
- Hectic, superficial breathing
- Cold ears and feet
- Pale skin (abdomen and inner thighs) and pale mucous membranes (mouth, eyes) and ears
- Apathy and anxiety

Epileptic seizure
A seizure can be very brief or rather long. The dog will fall over and stay lying in an abnormal position with convulsions. It may urinate, drool or have widened pupils.
After a seizure your dog will be exhausted and gasping from the exertion. The animal is dull and uncoordinated. An epileptic fit looks very serious and can cause panic in anyone witnessing it. With properly applied first aid, the whole situation is a lot less

serious than it looks. Therefore stay calm and proceed as follows:

- Carefully drag the dog by its back legs or body to a place where it cannot injure itself through its thrashing movements. For example, never leave it lying at the top of the stairs.
- Try to lessen the convulsions somewhat by putting a blanket or cloth over the animal and by surrounding it with cushions. This also decreases the risk of the animal injuring itself.
- Never try to apply a halter or hold the animal in a restraining grip. Also do not give your dog any food, water or medication (valium/diazepam suppositories).
- If necessary, apply mouth-to-mouth resuscitation. Watch your fingers when the dog starts breathing on its own again.
- Let the dog come round in a calm, dark environment. Stay and observe it for at least half an hour.
- If the seizures come back within a short interval, you are facing an emergency situation. Take the animal to the veterinarian as soon as possible.

Sunstroke

A dog may also be affected by heat. This often happens when the animal is left in a car for a long time, which is badly ventilated and standing in the sun.
Sunstroke (or heatstroke) can be recognised by the following symptoms: fast, jerky breathing, a glazed look and a body temperature of more than 40°C.

Take the animal to a shady, cool place. Immerse it in a bucket or tub of cold water or hose it down. Especially sparsely haired parts of the body, such as the belly, the elbows and the groin, need to be cooled off quickly. Stop with this when the body temperature drops below 39°C. When the animal comes to, you need to dry it off and let it drink small amounts of water in intervals of a few minutes. Take the victim to the veterinarian as soon as possible.

5. Poisoning

If an animal has been poisoned, a number of different symptoms might appear. It will often have breathing problems, it will feel cold to touch and it might lose consciousness. However, it might also be shaking and hyperactive. Always bear in mind that there is an increased chance of the animal going into shock.

Take the poison away from the dog as quickly as possible, but make sure that it does not become scared. Under no circumstances must the dog be frightened and run away. Remove any remnants of the poison from its mouth or the skin with a cloth as quickly as possible. Try to find out what the poison is. Take the package or whatever is left of the toxin to the veterinarian. This might be vital when it comes to determining the right antidote. How your dog has to be treated further depends on the type of poison it has ingested.

If your dog has ingested something from the group of 'non-caustic' substances (see table), you need to make it vomit as quickly as possible. You can stimulate vomiting by placing a teaspoon of salt on the back of its tongue. Pick up some of the sick with a plastic bag and take it to the veterinarian. If the dog is unconscious, lay its head lower than the rest of the body. This allows the vomit to flow out of its mouth and prevents it from flowing into the lungs. If necessary, apply mouth-to-mouth resuscitation. If the animal cannot be taken to a vet immediately, it is best to wrap it in a blanket and to take it to a dark, quiet place. Sometimes you can read on packages of toxins which substances need to be administered as antidotes. If the dog has thrown up properly, you can give it a mix of milk and Norit. This is advisable if it will take some time before you can take your dog to the veterinarian.

If your pet has ingested a 'caustic' substance (see table), it must not throw up under any circumstances! The mucous membranes of the mouth, throat and gullet have already been seriously damaged by the caustic toxin. If the toxin passes through them again, the damage will be more serious. Try to dilute the toxins in the digestive tract. In the case of a base toxin, give your dog vinegar or lemon juice. If you dog has ingested an acid, feed it soda or milk.

Non-caustic substances:
- Anti-freeze
- Bleach (chlorine)
- Carbamates
- Pesticides:
  - Strychnine
  - Crimidine
- Lead (paint and roof covering)
- Insecticides:
  - Parathion
  - Dichlorvos
- Snail poison

Caustic substances:
- Base
  - Caustic soda
  - Many paint or wallpaper strippers
- Petrol
- Petroleum
- Paint thinner
- Acids
  - Battery acid
  - Hydrochloric acid

6. Fractures

Unfortunately, dogs quite regularly have broken bones or fractures. The prominent cause of fractures is road traffic accidents, but a fall from great height, a bite by another animal or a gun shot wound may also lead to fractures. When applying first aid to fractures you need to be very careful, as the hard, sharp edges of the broken bone can easily damage tissues and organs.

We differentiate two types of fractures. In closed fractures the skin has not been damaged and the fractured parts are therefore not exposed to the air. In open fractures the fractured parts break out of the skin through the wound. This type of fracture can have serious consequences, as the very sensitive bone marrow can become infected by bacteria. Such an infection can make an animal seriously ill and will slow down the healing process of the fracture.

An open fracture is obviously easy to diagnose. In the case of a closed fracture this is a little more difficult. There are, however, some symptoms which indicate a fracture: pain, swelling, loss of function in the broken limb, abnormal position of the bone, abnormal mobility of the broken limb and a grating sound during movement. When you have clearly diagnosed a fracture, you should proceed as follows:

- Hold your dog in a restraining grip and let it calm down as much as possible at the scene of the accident.
- Be aware of shock symptoms. They may occur if your dog is in a lot of pain.
- Make sure that the broken leg lies on top.
- Do not pull on the leg and make sure that the fracture is as still as possible.
- If the lower part of the leg is broken and if you need to transport the animal quite a distance, apply a preliminary splint. This can be a straight piece of wood, a piece of carton or a rolled-up newspaper. Carefully apply cotton wool or a thick cloth around the leg. Then apply the splints at the sides of the leg, so that the joints above and under the fracture can no longer move.
- Fasten the splints with tape or bandages, but do not pull them too tight. It is only a matter of immobilising the fracture for the time of transport, so that it does not move.
- Carefully push a blanket or board under the dog and lift the animal up. Make sure that it lies as quietly as possible.
- Take the animal to the veterinarian straight away.

In the case of an open fracture you need to make sure that the animal does not lick or scratch at the fracture. Put plenty of sterile gauze or a clean cloth onto the wound, so that no dirt can get into it. Do not put any salve or iodine onto it, as this only increases the risk of infection. The vet will need to treat an open fracture further.

7. Digestive tract

Vomiting

It is quite normal that dogs sometimes eat grass and throw up. They do this when their stomach bothers them. Eating grass stimulates vomiting, which means that the dog discards its stomach contents.

If a dog throws up too often, something is definitely wrong. Throwing up can have different causes, such as infections, worms, eating too much, poisoning and metabolic disturbances. Take your dog to the veterinarian as quickly as possible if it is throwing up heavily, throwing up blood and if it has a swollen belly and has a very ill appearance.

If your dog throws up regularly, but does not appear sick otherwise, you can try out whether the symptoms disappear if you feed it easily digestible food and make an appointment with your vet. You sometimes need to feed your dog before bedtime to prevent so-called 'bile vomiting' in the morning. You can buy special, easily digestible food at your pet shop or veterinarian for such cases. Divide the food into several portions per day, for example every two to four hours. Then the stomach gets the ideal opportunity to digest the food. Also make sure that your dog has plenty of fresh drinking water available. When the throwing up has stopped completely, you can carefully switch back to normal feeding. Start by replacing ten percent of the diet food with normal food. The next day you replace twenty percent, and so forth until the diet is once again one hundred percent normal food. If the problems have not disappeared, you need to contact a vet.

Diarrhoea

When your dog's faeces are soft or watery, it is suffering from diarrhoea. This is a symptom of a disturbed digestion. This can have several causes, such as infection,

worms, eating bad or cold food or a sudden change in the diet. If the diarrhoea is bloody, or if it is combined with symptoms such as fever, vomiting and apathy, take your dog to the veterinarian as soon as possible.
If your dog is suffering from light diarrhoea without being ill in any other way, feed it an easily digestible diet to solve the problem. Your vet or pet shop will have special, easily digestible feeds. Divide the feed into several smaller portions per day and feed it until the symptoms disappear, then slowly go back to normal food. This is best done by replacing ten percent of the diet food by normal food on the first day. On the second day you replace twenty percent and so on until the dog's diet consists of only normal food again. Always contact your vet if the diarrhoea does not stop; do not wait too long!

8. Other injuries

Bruises

To control the swelling, you can cover a bruise with a towel soaked in cold water or with ice cubes wrapped in a towel.

Traffic Accident Trauma

If you see a dog being hit by a car, do not run to it heedlessly. The last thing anyone needs in such a situation is another traffic victim! Immediately contact a vet or a pet ambulance. Make sure that other drivers become aware of the victim by clearly marking the scene of the accident. If necessary, take the victim in a restraining grip, carefully check if there are any bleeding wounds and treat the victim for shock. Carefully cover the dog with a coat or blanket. Let it lay quietly until professional help arrives. It is very important that you do not move the victim, even if no blood and wounds are visible at first sight, as the dog may have suffered internal injuries. You must also therefore not give the dog anything to drink until it has been examined by a vet.

Footpad injury

If your dog is walking awkwardly or licking its paw, there might be a splinter or another object stuck in the sole of its foot. You can carefully remove this with tweezers. Disinfect the spot with iodine straight away and bandage it. This prevents the dog licking at the wound and thus infecting it. In the case of heavy blood loss, or if the object is stuck deep in the sole, you need to take your dog to the veterinarian.

Choking

Dogs like to play with all sorts of things. It can therefore happen that the animal swallows something by accident. This can be a number of different objects, with different consequences ranging from serious to less acute. In the worst case, the swallowed object is stuck just before the windpipe. The animal can no longer breathe and this is obviously a life-threatening situation. An object which ends up in the gullet causes discomfort and sometimes a lot of pain, but the dog will not die of it immediately. You can recognise that an object is stuck in the gullet by the dog swallowing frequently and trying to throw up. The dog will drool a lot and rub its snout. In this case, proceed as follows:

- Hold your dog in a restraining grip if it does not want to accept your help.
- The dog will usually vomit; giving it food or water will only make things worse.
- An object in the gullet is a nuisance, but not life-threatening. Therefore remain calm. If the object is close to the windpipe, the animal will be in danger, which means that you need to act quickly.

- Open its mouth as far as possible and look into its throat. If the sharp teeth make it difficult to hold the snout open, take a dry tissue to carefully pull out the tongue. The dog will keep its snout open, as it will not risk biting its tongue.
- If the object is clearly visible, you can carefully remove it with tweezers or small pliers. If an object is located just before the windpipe, you can sometimes remove it by putting a finger behind it, deep in the throat. Someone else will have to push on the right spot of the throat from the outside.
- If you do not succeed, lay the dog on its side on a hard surface.
- Apply pressure just behind the last ribs, where the thorax is widest. Push downwards and forwards with both hands. This sometimes makes the object shoot out of the throat.
- Repeat this action several times quickly one after another if you do not succeed the first time. If the object is still stuck in the throat, try removing the object from the throat with your fingers, while someone else continues pressing behind the ribs. If necessary, apply mouth-to-mouth resuscitation.
- If the object has not been removed within a few minutes, take your dog to the veterinarian as quickly as possible. Even if you did manage to remove the object, your vet will still need to examine your dog for possible complications, such as damage to the throat or gullet. Do not take any risks opening the dog's mouth or removing an object, watch your hands and fingers!

Your dog may have swallowed a sharp object, such as a splinter or a fish bone. They will usually get caught in the mucous membranes of the mouth. In this case your dog will rub its snout a lot with its paw. It will also salivate excessively, sometimes mixed with blood or retch. Some dogs might sit quietly in one corner, whereas others will run around the house like maniacs.

- Try to have a good look into your dog's throat. If necessary, apply a restraining grip.
- If you have localised the sharp object, you can carefully try to remove it. If it is stuck very tightly, leave it in the snout.
- Carefully wipe the froth from the oral cavity and take your dog to the veterinarian as quickly as possible.
- During your journey, hold onto your dog's paws, so that it cannot injure itself by continuously rubbing against its snout.
- Your vet will remove the object, probably under anaesthetic. After this, your dog will have some problems eating and will need to be fed an adjusted diet.

Wounds

A dog can become wounded in a number of ways. You may therefore encounter a wide range of wounds, which vary in their severity. Roughly, you can divide them into simple wounds, in which only the skin surface has been damaged and complex wounds, in which deeper layers, such as muscles, blood vessels and nerves have also been affected. Both types obviously need to be treated in their own way.

Always take your dog to the veterinarian if it has suffered a severe wound. Graze wounds are best cleaned with warm boiled water.

More danger

Our modern houses actually are a very strange environment for animals. There are no trees, no grass, and no shrubs. The wind does not blow around their ears. There is no stream with fresh water and no trees to scratch on. An animal needs to adapt. This does not always go smoothly, but we can make sure that its life with us is as safe as possible.

Plants

It is common knowledge that cats sometimes like to eat grass. Dogs do this too. You never know what a dog sees in a plant. Puppies in particular occassionally like to 'take a bite'. The likelihood is not big, but if it does happen, take your dog and a branch of the plant in question to your vet. He will know the best course of action. We will provide a short overview of toxic plants.

TOXIC PLANTS

-A-

Abrus precatorius - Precatory-pea
Acer rubrum - Red maple
Aconitum napellus - Monk's hood
Aesculus hippocastanum - Horse chestnut
Ailanthus altissima - Tree-of-heaven
Allamanda cathartica - Golden-trumper
Allium cepa - Onion
Allium sativum - Garlic
Alstroemeria ligtu - Peruvian lily
Amaranthus hybridus - Smooth pigweed
Amaryllis vittata - Amaryllis *(A. vittata)*
Anthurium andraenum - Flamingo lily
Aquilegia alpina - Aquilegia
Asimina triloba - Pawpaw

-B-

Baptista tinctoria - Wild indigo
Barbarea vulgaris - Yellow rocket
Buxus sempervirens - Buxus

-C-

Caladium bicolor - Caladium
Chrysanthemum indicum - Chrysanthemum
Cicuta virosa - Northern water-hemlock
Clematis - Clematis
Clivia miniata - Kaffir lily
Codiaeum variegetum - Croton
Colchicum autumnale - Autumn crocus
Conium macaltum - Poison-hemlock
Convallaria majalis - Lily-of-the-valley
Corydalis - Corydalis
Crocus - Crocus
Cyclamen persicum - Cyclamen

-D-

Dature innoxia - Angel's trumpet
Datura stramonium - Jimsomweed
Delphinium - Larkspur
Dieffenbachia seguine - Mother-in-law-plant
Digitalis purpurea - Foxglove

-E-

Euonymus europaeus - European spindletree
Euphorbia helioscopia - Sun spurge
Euphorbia lacteal - Candelabra-cactus
Euphorbia pulcherrima - Poinsettia

-F-

Fagopyrum esculentem - Tall manna grass

Aquilegia

Buxus

Clematis

Corydalis

Crocus

-G-

Gutierrezia sarothrae - Broom snakewood
Gymnocladus dioicus - Kentucky coffeetree

-H-

Hedera helix - English ivy
Helenium autumnale - Sneezeweed
Helianthus annuus - Sunflower
Heliotropium curassavicum - Spatulate-leaved heliotrope
Heracleum mantegazzianum - Giant hogweed
Humulus lupulus - Common hop
Hyancinthoides nonscripta - English bluebell
Hydrangea macrophylla - Hydrangea
Hypercum perforatum - St. John's wort

-I-

Ilex aquifolium - English holly
Ipomoea tricolour - Morning glory
Iris pseudocorus - Yellow iris
Iris versicolor - Blue flag iris

-J-

Juglans nigra - Black walnut

-K-

Kalanchoe daigremontiana - Devil's-backbone
Kalmia angustofolia - Sheep-laurel

-L-

Laportea canadensus - Canada nettle
Lathyrus odoratus - Sweet pea
Lathyrus sativus - Grass pea
Leonurus cardiaca - Motherwort
Ligistrum vulgare - Common privet
Linaria vulgaris - Yellow toadflax
Lobelia cardinalis - Cardinalflower
Lobelia inflate - Indian-tobacco
Lonicera xylosteum - Fly honeysuckle
Lupinus argenteus - Silvery lupine
Lupinus polyphyllus - Large-leaved lupine
Lupinus pusillus - Small lupine
Lupinus sericeus - Silky lupine

-M-

Mangifera indica - Mango
Medicago sativa - Alfalfa
Melilotus alba - White sweet clover
Melitus officinalis - Yellow sweet clover
Menispermum canadense - Moonseed
Monstera deliciosa - Swiss-cheese plant

-N-

Narcissus peoticus - Narcissus
Narcissus pseudonarcissus - Daffodil

Delphinium

Datura

Digitalis

Euonymus

Hedera

Hydrangea

Ilex

Lonicera

Nerium oleander - Oleander
Nicotiana tabacum - Tobacco

-O-
Onoclea sensibilis - Sensitive fern
Ornithogalum umbellatum - Star-of-Bethlehem
Oxytropus lambertii - Purple locoweed

-P-
Papaver nudicaule - Iceland poppy
Papaver orientale - Oriental poppy
Papaver somniferum - Opium poppy
Parthenocissus quinquefolia - Virginia creeper
Persea americana - Avocado
Phacelia campanularia - California canarygrass
Phalaris arundinacea - Reed canarygrass
Philodendron cordatum - Philodendron
Phoradendron flavescens - American mistletoe
Physalis alkekengi - Chinese-lantern
Physalis peruviana - Ground-cherry
Phytolacca american - Pokeweed
Pinus ponderosa - Ponderosa pine
Primula obconica - Primula
Polygonatum multiflorum - Solomon's seal
Prunus pennsylvanica - Pin cherry
Ptedidium aquilinum - Bracken

-Q-
Quercus alba - White oak
Quercus rubra - Red oak

-R-
Rananculus bulbosus - Bulbous buttercup
Raphanus raphanistrum - Wild radish
Raphanus sativus - Radish
Rhamnus carthartica - European buckthorn
Rheum rhaponticum - Rhubarb
Rhododendron macrophyllum - California rose-baby
Rhus diversiloba - Western poison-oak
Rhus radicans - Poison ivy
Ricinus communis - Castor-bean
Robinia pseudoacacia - Black locust
Rudbeckia serotina - Black-eyed Susan
Rumex acetosa - Garden sorrel

-S-
Sambucus canadensis - American elder
Sambucus nigra - European elder
Sarcobatus vermiculatus - Greasewood
Scilla siberica - Siberian scilla
Senecop jacobaea - Tansy ragwort
Sinapis arvensis - Wild mustard
Solanum dulcamara - Climbing nightshade
Solanum nigrum - Black nightshade
Solanum speudocapsicum - Jerusalem-cherry

Lupinus

Papaver orientalis

Parthenocissus

Phytolacca

Polygonatum

Rhododendron

Solanum tuberosum	- Potato
Solidago mollis	- Velvety goldenrod
Sorghum halepense	- Johnson grass
Suckleya suckleyana	- Poison suckleya
Symphoricarpos albus	- Thin-leaved snowberry
Symphytum asperum	- Prickly comfrey
Symplocarpus foetidus	- Skunk cabbage
-T-	
Tanacetum vulgare	- Tansy
Taxus canadensis	- Canada yew
Thermopsis rhombifolia	- Golden-bean
Thlaspi arvense	- Stinkweed
Thuja	- Thuja
Trifolium pratense	- Red clover
Trifolium repens	- White clover
Tulipa gesneriana	- Tulip
-U-	
Urica dioica	- Stinging nettle
-V-	
Veratrum viride	- False hellebore
Viburnum opulus	- Guelder-rose
Vicia sativa	- Common vetch
-W-	
Wisteria floribunda	- Japanese wisteria
-X-	
Xanthium strumarium	- Cocklebur
-Z-	
Zigadenus elegans	- White camas

Ricinus

Sedum spectabile

Thuja

Other dangers

A human walks on two legs and does not always see what can happen at ankle and knee height. You could say that anything that may be dangerous for a crawling baby can also be dangerous for a dog. We will give you a few examples.

Cables

Young dogs like to bite into all sorts of things. Wires from lamps, the computer and other electric appliances can be found everywhere in the house. Hide these as far as possible. You can also buy certain materials to wrap around cables and thus protect them.

Detergents

Although most people do not think of detergents as being immediate hazards for dogs, they contain substances which are toxic for dogs. So it is self-explanatory that you should not let your dog walk over them or spray it with detergents, but danger is still lurking around the corner. Just take simple mopping of the floor, something you will have to do more regularly if you have pets. Whichever cleaning equipment you use, at a certain point the floor is wet while you are working. If the dog walks over the wet floor, it will also get detergent on its paws. If the dog licks its paws dry again it will then still ingest toxic detergent.

Chocolate

Sometimes we think that what we see on television is actually true. In cartoons, but also in some programmes, there is a strange notion of dogs and sweets. Do not be tempted to think that what dogs eat in cartoons is actually the right food for dogs in real life. Chocolate is one of those products that humans enjoy, but which is actually toxic for dogs and cats. Chocolate contains certain substances which their bodies cannot break down. So never feed a dog chocolate and definitely do not let it scavenge around. Luckily, most cats do not like sweet food, but dogs do!

Tips

- A Shih Tzu is a soft-natured dog that won't respond well to a harsh hand.
- Ignore submissive or anxious behaviour; certainly don't comfort your dog.
- A Shih Tzu can be somewhat cocky; a rigorous and consequent, but not harsh, upbringing is very important!
- Attend a puppy course with your dog. You will both benefit.
- Visit a number of breeders before buying a puppy.
- The Shih Tzu is an energetic dog. It will find dog sports great fun, but don't take them too seriously!
- Its first trip in a car is a real experience for a puppy; make it a pleasant one.
- Check your Shih Tzu's coat for tangles regularly. Often give your dog a good brush throughout!
- Do not just fight the fleas, but the larvae too.
- Taking your dog with you on holiday? It is the best thing you can do.
  However, make sure that your Shih Tzu will be welcome before you go.
- Hard chunks and plenty to chew on will ensure healthy teeth.
- Never buy a puppy if you have been unable to see its mother.
- Clean your dog's eyes each day.
- A puppy will mean a lot of work, and sometimes a few grey hairs.
- Get in touch with the breed association for the address of a reliable Shih Tzu breeder.
- Take care that your dog does not get too fat. Not too much food and plenty of exercise is the rule.
- Ask to see the parent dogs' papers.
- Never buy a Shih Tzu on impulse.
- Never let a small dog be unattended on a high table or on a chair. It can hurt itself badly when it wants to jump down.
- Never let your puppy run endlessly after a ball or stick.
- Do not add supplements to ready-made foods.
- Never allow your Shih Tzu puppy to run up and down stairs for the first six months!
- A Shih Tzu will be quiet at home if it's allowed to work off its energy outdoors.
- Allow your Shih Tzu to rest after meals.

Internet

A great deal of information can be found on the internet. A selection of websites with interesting details and links to other sites and pages is listed here. Sometimes pages move to another site or address. You can find more sites by using the available search engines.

For Great Britain

www.theshihtzuclub.co.uk
The Shih Tzu Club - UK is dedicated to the promotion, welfare and improvement of Shih Tzu dogs in the United Kindom. The club holds three shows per year for Shih Tzu lovers. The aims and objectives of the club are:

1. To maintain the Kennel Club standard of the Shih Tzu in the UK.
2. To promote and protect the interests of all Shih Tzu.
3. To help encourage and advise all Shih Tzu owners.

www.manchushihtzusociety.co.uk
The Manchu Shih Tzu Society was established during the time that there was a great variation in size. A smaller type was appearing in some bloodlines and the genes for smallness had also been introduced through several imported lines.

www.shihtzuclubscotland.co.uk
Although this club is one of the younger clubs of the breed, the Shih Tzu dog has had a long association with Scotland.

www.ncshihtzuclub.co.uk
As a Kennel Club registerd Breed Club, which was established in 1981, Northern Counties Shih Tzu Clubs' primary objective is being proactive in the preservation and protection of the Shih Tzu as defined in the Kennel Club Breed Standard in the UK.

www.walesandweststc.co.uk
The Shih Tzu Club of South Wales and Western Counties. Popularly known as 'The Wales and West', whose primary focus is the area from the West Midlands down to Cornwall in England and most of Wales.

www.southernshihtzurescue.org.uk
Southern Shih Tzu Rescue is a UK registered charity dealing with the rescue and re-homing of Shih Tzu dogs.

www.homecounties-shihtzurescue.co.uk
This rescue was started up in 1996 from nothing, just wanting to help unwanted dogs and trying to make a difference. Now it has established a good reputation for re-homing dogs and one-on-one basis to help dogs recover, with a very holistic approach to their future lives.

www.pet-insurance-uk.me.uk
Find low cost pet insurance via this UK insurance directory.

www.pethealtcare.co.uk.
At pethealthcare.co.uk they believe that a healthy pet is a happy pet. Which is why they have brought together leading experts to create a comprehensive online source of pet care information.

www.onlinepetcare.co.uk
www.onlinepetcare.co.uk was launched in 2001 and contains information about and links to businesses and charities in the Midlands area involved in the care and purchasing of domestic animals.

http://champdogs.co.uk
Search the champ dogs database for kennels, stud dogs and litters.

http://dogtraining.co.uk
Your central resource for dog-training, boarding kennels & vets in the UK.

www.k9magazine.com
This refreshing magazine is produced with today's conscientious dog owner in mind and provides a fascinating insight into the latest news, views and gossip from the UK and world dog scene as well as an easy access point to valuable advice, tips and expert opinions from some of the world's leading pet authorities.

www.rspca.org.uk
The Royal Society for the Prevention of Cruelty to Animals. If you are interested in re-homing a dog (or other animal) pay a visit to your local RSPCA animal centre. This site provides information on animal care.

www.mypetstop.com
An international, multi-lingual website with information on keeping, breeding, behaviour, healthrelated issues and much more.

www.waltham.com
Waltham is a firm specialized in pet care and nutrition. On this website you can find more information on pet care, training and diets.

www.the-kennel-club.org.uk
The Kennel Club's primary objective is to promote, in every way, the general improvement of dogs. This site aims to provide you with information you may need to be a responsible pet owner and to help you keep your dog happy, safe and content.

www.k9-care.co.uk
The Self-Help site for dog owners. A beautiful website with tons of information on dogs. All you need to know about grooming, training, health care, buying a dog, travel and much more.

European Shih Tzu Clubs

www.shih-tzu-club.de
This is the German Shih Tzu Club as well as the International Shih Tzu Club. The International Shih Tzu Club was established in 1980, it is a member of VDH (German Kennel Club) and FCI and it is a very special club for the Shih Tzu breed.

www.kolumbus.fi/shihtzury
This is the site of the Finnish Shih Tzu Club, it was established in 1971. Several interesting articles are written in the Englisch language.

www.shih-tzu.se
Special Club for Shih Tzu in Sweden. A highly interesting site, unfortunately only in Swedish, but with a remarkable list of links.

www.shihtzuclub.nl
The site of the Shih Tzu Club in the Netherlands.

www.chienstibetains.com
This is the site of the official French association responsible for the Tibetan breeds in France. Unfortunately the site is only in the French language.

www.shihtzu.no
This site contains the Chinese standard from 1938.

www.shihtzuhundar.com
The Shih Tzu Club from Iceland. The site is also in the English language.

For U.S.A.

www.shihtzu.org
The site of the American Shih Tzu Club.

www.shihtzuclubofsewi.org
The site of the Shih Tzu Club of Southeastern Wisconsin USA.

www.stfsc.bizland.com
The site of the Shih Tzu Fanciers of Southern CA.

www.shih-tzu-fanciers.com
The site of Puget Sound Shih Tzu Fanciers US.

www.aboutpets.info
The website of the publisher of the About Pets book series. An overview of the titles, availability in which languages and where in the world the books are sold.

Worldwide Shih Tzu Clubs

www.geocities.com/Petsburgh/Haven/9556/index.html
The site of the Australian Shih Tzu Club of Victoria.

www.canadianshihtzuclub.ca
The site of the Canadian Shih Tzu Club.

www.geocities.com/philshihtzuclub
The Philippine Shih Tzu Club. This site is written in the English language.

Addresses

Becoming a member of a breed association or club can be very useful for good advice and interesting activities. A Shih Tzu club will give you the opportunity to meet other Shi Tzu lovers. Contact The Kennel Club in case addresses or telephone numbers have changed.

The Kennel Club
1 – 5 Clarges Street
Picadilly
London WIJ 8AB
Tel.: 0870 606 6750
Fax: 020 7518 1058
www.thekennelclub.org.uk

Scottish Kennel Club
Eskmills Park Station Road
Musselburgh
Edinburgh EH21 7PQ
Tel.: 0131 665 3920
Fax: 0131 653 6937
www.scottishkennelclub.org
E-mail: info@scottishkennelclub.org

The Irish Kennel Club LTD
Fottrell House
Harolds X Bridge,
Dublin 6W
Ireland
Tel.: +353 (1) 4533 300 – 4532 309 – 4532 310
Fax: +353 (1) 4533 237
www.ikc.ie
E-mail: ikenclub@indigo.ie

Breed associations

Becoming a member of a breed association can be very useful for good advice and interesting activities.

Shih Tzu Club Uk
E-mail: secretary@theshihtzuclub.co.uk
www.theshihtzuclub.co.uk/

Manchu Shih Tzu Society
E-mail:
secretary@manchushihtzusociety.co.uk
www.manchushihtzusociety.co.uk

Shih Tzu Club of Scotland
E-mail: shihtzuscotland@tiscali.co.uk
www.shihtzuclubscotland.co.uk/

Northern Counties Shih Tzu Club
E-mail: denise@paliden.co.uk
www.ncshihtzuclub.co.uk

Shih Tzu Club of South Wales and Western Countries
www.walesandweststc.co.uk

For U.S.A.

American Kennel Club
The AKC provides coverage on all accepted breeds. Gives information on registration, pedigrees and dog shows. Look at the website! So much to see about breeders, breeds, registration, addresses and events.
www.akc.org

United Kennel Club
The United Kennel Club was established in 1998. It is the largest all-breed performance-dog registry in the world, registering dogs from all 50 states and 25 foreign countries.
UKC
100 E Kilgore Rd Kalamazoo MI
49002 – 5584
Office hours: 09:00 to 16:30 (E.S.T.)
Monday trough Friday.
Tel.: 269 – 343 – 9020
Fax: 269 – 343 – 7037

Profile

Name:	Shih Tzu
Group:	Utility Group
Origin:	Tibet
First breed standard:	Great Britain 1935
Original use:	Toy-dog and companion-dog.
Use today:	They are bred for showing and to keep as a pet.
Height:	Height is not important
Weight:	4.5 to 8.1 kgs
Life expectancy (average):	10 - 12 years